The Diplomacy of a New Age

THE DIPLOMACY
OF A NEW AGE

MAJOR ISSUES IN U.S. POLICY
SINCE 1945

by Dexter Perkins

The United States in the nineteenth century was a provincial nation that rarely looked beyond the New World. Its military forces were small and its influence in European affairs negligible. Today the United States owns one of the largest armed establishments in the world and has interests and power in every quarter of the globe. What produced this striking change? What events transformed a traditionally isolationist people into a nation of unparalleled international influence? What are the implications for the future? These are some of the questions which Dexter Perkins considers in this survey of the major events in United States foreign policy since World War II.

The volume presents close analyses of several areas of international affairs. In clarifying the pattern of Soviet-American relations, Mr. Perkins examines the key sources of conflict: the disposition of Germany after the war, the creation of Russian satellites in eastern Europe, the sending of military aid to Greece, and the West Berlin blockade and airlift. He notes that the Marshall Plan, described by Winston Churchill as "the most unsordid act" in history, owes its existence to the spread of Keynesian economic theory and new international monetary systems. The North Atlantic Treaty Organization, the first peacetime alliance explicitly committing the United States to the use of armed force, is, in Mr. Perkins' view, "one of the many auguries of a more integrated Western society."

Evaluating America's role in Asia, Mr. Perkins reviews the Korean conflict, the record of American diplomacy in China, and the ques-

(continued on back flap)

(continued from front flap)

tion of admitting Red China to the United Nations. Concerning the United States' relations with Latin America, he observes both signs of solidarity and potentially divisive forces, and assesses the overt challenges of Communism in Guatemala and Cuba.

The salient fact of the past thirty years, Mr. Perkins concludes, is the United States' development of massive economic and military power and expanding global commitments. He believes that on the whole this country has made creditable use of its influence and finds both encouraging and disheartening aspects to such urgent questions as the future of Soviet-American relations, the role of the United Nations as peacemaker, the international control of nuclear weapons, and the needs of emerging nations. We in America cannot hope to evade our responsibilities; rather, in Mr. Perkins' words, "We shall have to face the grave problems of the international society with enlarged knowledge, with chastened judgment, and with resolution."

(INDIANA UNIVERSITY INTERNATIONAL STUDIES)

The
Diplomacy
of a New Age

Major Issues in U. S. Policy
since 1945

Dexter Perkins

INDIANA UNIVERSITY PRESS
Bloomington and London

THE PATTEN FOUNDATION

Mr. Will Patten of Indianapolis (A.B., Indiana University, 1893) made, in 1931, a gift for the establishment of the Patten Foundation at his Alma Mater. Under the terms of this gift, which became available upon the death of Mr. Patten (May 3, 1936), there is to be chosen each year a Visiting Professor who is to be in residence several weeks during the year. The purpose of this prescription is to provide an opportunity for members and friends of the University to enjoy the privilege and advantage of personal acquaintance with the Visiting Professor. The Visiting Professor for the Patten Foundation in 1966 was

DEXTER PERKINS

Contents

Preface

The student of American foreign policy since 1945 must inevitably be aware of the pitfalls in his path. On the one hand, the printed materials are so voluminous that it would take a lifetime to exhaust them. On the other hand, the vital diplomatic correspondence has for the most part not yet seen the light of day. Even our own government, the most generous in informing its citizens of the course of diplomacy, is far from publishing all the important exchanges of views that take place. In addition to all this, no one who has worked in the field of diplomatic history can fail to realize how perspective changes, or how suddenly fresh events compel a re-evaluation of the data. The death of a statesman, the fortunes of an election, the overturn of a government, economic disaster, or the effects of prosperity, all may have a fundamental effect on the course of events. The realization of this fact suggests that opinions of a general character must be held provisionally, and that the scholar must always be ready to re-evaluate his data.

Yet it would be foolish, on this account, not to seek to find some pattern in the vast web of events. The specialist must be modest, but he may hope that he can provide some insights that will be useful, some views more penetrating than that of the novice. It is with this point of view in mind that this book has been written.

This book springs from an invitation to give at Indiana University the Patten Lectures for 1966. To those who extended the invitation, and especially to Professor Hubert C. Heffner, the chairman of the committee, and Professor Robert H. Ferrell, who welcomed me with special warmth, I am very grateful. To Professor Leo F. Solt, the chairman of the History Department, and to his colleagues, I owe much of the pleasure I derived from my visit to Bloomington. There were many other persons, too numerous to mention, who made my stay there memorable.

The manuscript was prepared for the press with the assistance of Mrs. William G. Doe, of Harvard, Massachusetts. I gratefully acknowledge her efficient aid.

DEXTER PERKINS

The Diplomacy of a New Age

ONE

The Growing Rift

In the course of the last twenty years the United States has attained a place of power among the nations that has no parallel in history. It possesses one of the largest armed establishments in the world; and to this establishment must be added its awesome array of nuclear weapons, carrying with it a power of destruction that baffles the imagination. It has interests, and carries weight, in almost every quarter of the globe—in Europe, in Asia, in Latin America. It is today far removed from the provincial nation that during the nineteenth century rarely looked beyond the area of the New World, and sought to insulate itself against the wiles of foreign influence. In this little book I propose to examine how this came about, and to trace the implications of this monumental change for our own country, and for the rest of the world.

With regard to sheer physical power, it is fair to say that no one could have dreamed even a quarter of a century ago of the position we occupy today. For the greater part of its history the United States was content with a very modest military establishment. Standing armies were thought to be dangerous to liberty; a modest navy was considered to be sufficient to protect the commercial interests of the United States. At the outset of the war of 1812, the total land forces of the United States amounted to some 12,000 men. At the time of the Mexican War, the figure was 7,400 men. The vast armies raised in the Civil War were speedily dissolved, and by 1890, the regular army had shrunk to a mere 27,000 men. It was scarcely larger at the time of the outbreak of the war with Spain. Even in the twentieth century, our peace-time land forces were ridiculously small. In the First World War, we mustered a large force, of 3,500,000 men. But when the war was over, that force was speedily dissolved. By the end of the 1919 the figure was shrinking rapidly. "Get the boys home, toot sweet," was the masthead on the *Chicago Tribune* which I used to read at Chaumont, our General Headquarters, in the winter following the armistice. By 1935 our military forces had shrunk to 137,000 and they were only 269,000 on the verge of the Second World War. Again, in the emergency, we raised colossal forces, over 11,000,000 in the army alone. But again we dissolved those forces when the conflict was over. By 1946 the number was in the neighborhood of 500,000.

Not only this, but Americans, speaking in historical terms, have shown a very real dislike for compulsory military service. The early American conflicts were fought with volunteers. In the Civil War, a struggle for national existence, the draft was adopted only in 1863, and then applied in such a way as to make it very far from universal in practice. It was not until 1917, and only after the war had begun, that the country accepted the principle of conscription, and with peace the old reliance on volunteer forces was revived. In the Second World War, the government moved more rapidly, and the first conscription act in time of peace was enacted in the summer of 1940. But in 1941, when extension of this legislation was proposed, the House of Representatives approved this extension by a single vote. Nor does the United States have universal training today. It depends to a substantial degree upon volunteers, with the draft as a distinctly secondary measure of recruitment. No one can fairly speak of the United States as a militarized nation.

What has been true of the armed forces has been true of the naval forces as well. The United States began its career as a nation without any navy at all. Though there was some progress in developing a substantial force in the decades that followed, and though the American navy gave a good account of itself in the War of 1812, it was not until the Civil War that a really powerful navy came into being. With the end of the war, the country reverted into something like complete impotence. By the 1880's the tide began to turn, and by the time of the First World War the United States was one of the foremost naval powers of the world. But characteristically, at the end of the struggle, there came about an attempt to limit naval forces by agreement, in the treaties of Washington (1922) and London (1930). Nor did we even build up to the agreed limits until some years later.

Moreover, reviewing their history as a whole, the American people have shown certainly as much interest as the people of any great nation in building the machinery of peace. It might even be argued that they have shown a somewhat exaggerated faith in this regard. In this first decades of the century there was a great—perhaps an excessive—belief in the development of international law; the American government played a central role in the drafting of the Covenant of the League of Nations, and notable Americans supported the League, even after it had been rejected by the Senate; American public opinion prodded a reluctant administration into the negotiation of the Kellogg-Briand pact, which outlawed war as an instrument of national policy; and American opinion enthusiastically supported the creation of the United Nations at the end of the Second World War. Nothing in the American past suggests the preoccupation with power that distinguished the France of Napoleon or the Germany of Adolf Hitler.

How has it come about, then, that in the years since 1945 this country has trod the path of other great nations, and fashioned a power structure of immense dimensions and far-reaching influence? Before we answer that question, we should say that such developments were hardly foreseen in 1944, or even in 1945. It is fair to state that while the Second World War was still being fought a great many Americans (including the author of this study) were disposed to believe in the possibility of an understanding with the colossus of the Kremlin. The war had brought together the Soviet Union and the United States as allies; the dramatic meeting of the great war leaders at Teheran at the end of 1943 seemed to augur well for the future, and the conference at Yalta in 1945, whatever may be the judgment of it today, was at the time widely regarded as a confirmation of that unity which had been affirmed in the capital of Iran. A public opinion poll of March 1945 revealed that more than half of the persons interrogated believed in the possibilities of co-operation with Russia in the years ahead; of the 100 percent polled, making allowances for the 14 per cent who remained undecided, the vote was almost two to one in favor of a hopeful judgment of the future.

We can readily see why this was true. While many Americans have sometimes had a naive faith in the universal applicability of the democratic ideal, it has not been characteristic of them to nourish positive hostility toward regimes of another form. Among intellectuals the Fascist regime of Mussolini aroused antagonism, but the relations of the United States with the Italian government were not seriously damaged by the difference in form. In the same way, official policy had usually tolerated authoritarian regimes in Latin America. And in the beginning, even Adolf Hitler aroused no great repugnance. Indeed, one of the most respected of American commentators hailed the advent of the Fuehrer to power as a sign of national regeneration in Germany. It was only with the persecution of the Jews that opinion began to change. Even at the time of Munich, in 1938, when the sinister purposes of the National Socialistic regime were becoming clear, there was no deep-seated and general hostility to the Third Reich. It is not strange, therefore, that even in 1945 there seemed to be some possibility, in the view of many Americans, for understanding with the Kremlin. The attitude of the publicists was matched, to some degree, by the attitude of statesmen. As late as the autumn of

1944, Averell Harriman, the devoted and able American ambassador at Moscow, could write optimistically of the future. To the day of his death, Franklin Roosevelt expressed the belief that though there might be difficulties with the Russians, matters would "straighten out."

In reality, however, and with the benefit of retrospect, we can see that there existed a deep divergence between the views of Washington and the views of Moscow. That divergence lay in the ideological sphere, and was the more ominous on that account. It is the sad story of diplomacy that while specific interests can be compromised, disputes in the field of ideas are extremely difficult of solution. The dreams of men have often influenced policy, and the dreams of the United States, on the one hand, and of the Communists on the other, presented, as we can now see, a massive obstacle to understanding. The revolutionary faith that had been kindled into flame in the great revolution of 1917 still burned brightly in Russia. Men who had participated in that revolution still stood at the levers of control, and cherished the hope that the war of 1939 to 1945 would undermine the old order in the West, and pave the way for the triumph of Communist principles. The grim monarch—for monarch he may be called—who dominated the Russian scene, filled with suspicion of his allies, and without scruples as to means, looked forward, at the least, to the extension of Russian power, and of the Communist faith. Cautious as to methods he might sometimes be; but tenacious as to ends he always was.

On the American side, despite the superficial optimism of the war years, there was bound to be a deep antagonism to the Kremlin. No political and economic philosophy, indeed, has ever aroused in the United States quite so deep a distrust as has Communism. The totalitarianism of the right, repulsive as it was to democratic idealists, left standing a large part of the economic order—even though it sought to control it. Communism, on the other hand, challenged that order in a funda-

mental way. The business classes could hardly fail to view
with intense repugnance a system of economic organization
which regards them as superfluous, as exploiters, as the source
and root of all economic evil. But it was not only the American
conservatives who found much to condemn in Communism.
The Soviet system violated also the tenets of American lib-
eralism. It was contemptuous of the individual; it placed no
value on human freedom; it prostituted knowledge to the
service of the state. It might be true that the welfare of the
masses was the objective of the Kremlin (though this might
be debated), but granted that this was so, was it worth the
price of a bloody tyranny that used the concentration camp
and the secret police to maintain itself in power, and which,
ignoring the possibilities of social adjustment in which Americans believed, proclaimed, now stridently, now cautiously, but
steadily, the necessity of a world revolution?

Still a third factor was to be taken into account, the bitter
hostility with which the Communists looked upon religion. In
particular, this affronted the Catholic population of the United
States, but the feeling was not confined to Catholics. Marxian
materialism seemed to many persons a threat both to the ideals
and to the vested interests of the church, and the devotees of
every religious group were antagonized by the fact that religion
in Russia was not free, but was, at best, the subservient tool of
the state.

Taking all these considerations together, it is not difficult to
understand what actually occurred. It is only the romantic,
or a certain type of professional diplomatist, who believes that
clearly defined self-interest governs the intercourse of nations.
The roots of diplomacy are to be found in feeling, feeling often
rationalized by the appropriate symbols, but feeling none the
less. To understand this fact is the business of every student of
foreign policy.

It is also true, however, with regard to Russo-American
relations, that knowledgeable people could find many specific

aspects of Communist foreign policy that, given their pre-
possessions, they might disapprove.

The Soviet regime was recognized only in 1933. In the years
that followed it violated many of its engagements, and presented anything but an alluring picture to the State Department. The cynical bargain with Hitler for the partition of
Poland which preceded the German invasion of that country
could hardly fail to antagonize many Americans. The invasion
of Finland in 1939 seemed to the people of the United States
an act of ruthless aggression. The absorption of the Baltic
states by the Soviet Union in 1940-41 was hardly to be viewed
with gratification in Washington. The churlishness—or at any
rate, the suspicion—with which the Russian ambassador in the
capital received warnings of Hitler's purpose to attack Russia
was undeniably irritating. It is true that in 1941, through the
ruthless folly of the Japanese militarists, the United States
found itself the ally of the Kremlin. But in the course of the
struggle itself there was plenty of evidence of the difficulty of
getting along with Stalin and his friends. Averell Harriman,
who, as we have seen, began his mission in Moscow in a mood
of hopefulness, had altered his view by 1945.

At the great conference of the Allies at Yalta in January-
February, 1945, the differences within the alliance were pa-
pered over, and the contemporary reaction was that remarkable
harmony had been achieved; but it was not long before the
scene changed.

One episode, occurring in March, 1945, reveals in a stark
light the congenital suspicion with which the Soviet Union
regarded its allies. On the Italian front the German High Command made overtures for surrender. Field Marshal Alexander,
accordingly, despatched representatives to discuss terms. There
was no thought of commitments in which the Russians would
have no voice. But the Kremlin was much aroused. First came
a violent protest from Molotov. Despite reassurances from
Roosevelt, Stalin on April 3 told the President, "My military

colleagues . . . do not have any doubts that the negotiations have taken place, and that they have ended in an agreement with the Germans, on the basis of which the German Commander on the Western Front—Marshal Kesselring—has agreed to open the front and permit the Anglo-American troops to advance to the East, and the Anglo-Americans have promised in return to ease for the Germans the peace terms." And then, a still sharper accusation, "As a result of this, at the present moment the Germans on the Western front have ceased to wage war against England and the United States. At the same time, the Germans continue the war with Russia, the ally of England and the United States."

It is no wonder that Roosevelt answered this communication with a protest against the "vile misrepresentations" which it contained. With Alexander's withdrawal of his representatives from contact with the Germans the tension was reduced, but the episode remained a dramatic reminder of the difficulties ahead.

Once again, in retrospect, what we are about to describe seems in no way remarkable. It might have been expected, having regard to the history of diplomacy in the past, that whatever fell within the sphere of Russian military power would be dealt with on the basis of that power, with little consideration for the feelings of the Western powers. It was, perhaps, naive to imagine that it could be otherwise. But at Yalta the Russians had signed the so-called Declaration of Liberated Europe, a declaration drawn up by the State Department itself, which pledged the Russian, British, and American governments "to form interim governments broadly representative of all democratic elements in the population, and pledged to the earliest possible establishment of free elections responsive to the will of the people, and to facilitate the holding of such elections." The pledge, it is true, was watered down by the proviso that such action would be taken whenever in the judgment of the three powers conditions so required, and Stalin may have thought of this proviso as giving the necessary escape from embarrassing commitments. None the less, it was disconcerting to find within weeks of the meeting in the Crimea that Mr. Vishinsky, the Russian deputy foreign minister, arrived in Bucharest, the capital of Rumania, demanded the resignation of the existing ministry, and installed in power a government dominated by Communists.

More troubling was the Russian action in Poland. Here, too, the Kremlin seemed on the way to establishing a Communist-dominated regime. Ruthlessly and thoroughly, it was eliminating the elements in Poland that were likely to oppose its purposes. It had set up a government in Poland that was largely composed of its sympathizers. It seemed unlikely that it intended to honor the Declaration of Liberated Europe, to which we have already alluded. Indeed, when Molotov, the Russian foreign minister, was on his way to the conference of San Francisco, he had an interview with President Truman, who had just succeeded to the office, in which he was sharply scolded for the failure of the Kremlin to keep its engagements; in fact he declared that on this occasion he had been talked to as he never had been before in his life. A tenacious and resolute man, it is not likely that Molotov left the presidential presence with a more sincere desire for reconciliation than when he entered it.

The episodes we have been describing, however, took place while the war was still in progress, and were, no doubt, unnoticed by many Americans. What Americans saw in that momentous spring of 1945 was the near approach of peace in Europe and the great conference in San Francisco that was to result in the drafting of the Charter of the United Nations. We shall have occasion from time to time to refer to the United Nations in what follows. Those who regard it as useless are as misguided as those who think of it as a universal solvent for the world of humanity. But one observation must be made here. The veto given to the great powers in the Security Council, a

veto apparently as much desired by the United States as by
the Soviet Union, seriously crippled the new organization as
an agency for *enforcing* peace. However necessary it may have
been (and it *was* necessary, probably, to ensure ratification of
the Charter by the Senate of the United States), its existence implied, from the outset, the desire of the two great states to
protect their interests from international coercion.

The drafting of the Charter had not been completed when
the resistance of the Germans was brought to an end, and
the German tyrant perished in the bunker at Berlin. We need
to note the circumstances under which the collapse took place.
At a much earlier date, it had been decided that Germany
should be placed under international occupation. In eastern
Germany a large zone was marked out for the Russians. Berlin
was placed under international control. These arrangements
had seemed reasonable enough at the time at which they were
made. At that time the Western powers had not even reached
the Rhine. They were not to do so until the early spring of
1945. In the meantime the Russians were advancing into Germany. The bargain did not seem to be a bad one. None the
less the fact is that the agreement paved the way for the
Communization of East Germany, and in doing so, prepared
the way for the vexing problems of the German future that are
still with us today.

When the representatives of the three great powers met at
Potsdam, in August of 1945, the centrifugal problems that
attend victory in the case of every alliance were sure to make
themselves felt. The Russians had fixed the frontier between
defeated Germany and Poland by unilateral acts, not waiting
for the decision of a peace conference, and they had riposted
to complaints of their support of the governments in eastern
Europe with attacks on the government of Greece, and on the
elections that had been held there under the aegis of the
British armed forces. They had made it clear that they wished
to install themselves at Constantinople, and exercise with a

subservient Turkey the control of the Dardanelles. With what must have seemed like effrontery to the representatives of the West, at Potsdam, when the disposition of the Italian colonies came under discussion, Molotov suggested that Tripolitania be placed under a Russian mandate. And with regard to Germany, not only had the Kremlin already begun the removal of large amounts of machinery and other goods, but it had reiterated a claim made as early as Yalta for staggering sums from Germany in reparations.

At the same time a new question arose that illustrates beautifully the realities of international intercourse. The Americans had insisted at Yalta and at Potsdam in interesting themselves in the fate of eastern Europe. Yet when in August there came about the collapse of Japan, the American government would not hear of any real interference with its treatment of Nippon. It is true that it agreed to the creation of an advisory council— but this council was to have no power but that of recommendation. For all practical purposes, the governance of Japan was placed in the hands of an American general, and a general whose subsequent career suggests a massive resistance to interference. To the Russian mind, it must have seemed that what was sauce for the goose was sauce for the gander, and that their policies in eastern Europe were no different in principle from American policies in Japan.

In one sense, of course, this was true. But it was true only if we regard with strict impartiality the Russian and the American dream. This most Americans—including this author—are not prepared to do.

In the autumn of 1945, however, the breach between the West and the East was still by no means complete. No doubt the Kremlin watched with satisfaction the precipitate demobilization of the American armed forces; no doubt it still hoped that the end of the war would result in an economic collapse in the United States; no doubt it hoped for economic disorganization in western Europe, but its policy was essentially cautious. After all, an adventurous course of action would have been folly after an exhausting war. Perhaps one may also say that it would have been inconsistent with the general temper of Russian policy, which, historically considered, has been selfish, intriguing, and devious, but rarely rash.

It still took some months before the sharpness of the cleavage between the West and the Soviet Union became crystal clear, and on occasion a conciliatory gesture on the part of the United States offered some faint hope of understanding.

In December, Secretary Byrnes went to Moscow. Though there were plenty of warm discussions, there seemed also to be a substantial area of agreement. The Russians accepted an American plan for a conference to draw up peace treaties with the states that had been associated with Germany in the war. They accepted American views on Japan. Understandings were arrived at with regard to the governments constituted in Rumania and Bulgaria. The secretary came back from the Russian capital convinced that the log jam had been broken.

But the success of the Moscow conference was illusory. Stalin did not hide from Byrnes the suspicion that the United States and Great Britain were secretly working together. His view must have been confirmed by the signing at the end of the year of an agreement providing for a substantial loan for Britain, while a Russian tentative proposal for a credit got "lost" somewhere in the State Department. Worse still, the first meeting of the Security Council of the United Nations at London in January, 1946, brought the Kremlin and the American government into collision. During the war the Russians and the Americans had put troops into Iran. The Russians were still there when the Council convened. The Iranian government brought a complaint against the Russians, charging "interference in the internal affairs of Iran." The United States and Great Britain supported the complaint. Though the question was temporarily settled by a resolution requesting the two governments to settle the question by negotiation, the discussion infuriated the Russians. They responded with a series of attacks on the West, assailing the conduct of the British in Greece and Indonesia, and supporting the demands of the Syrians and the Lebanese for the withdrawal of French troops from their territory. The tone of the debate was bitter, especially when Mr. Vishinsky, the Russian vice foreign minister, who had a special talent for invective, was involved. In striking fashion the divergence of views between the West and the Soviet Union was called to the attention of the people of the democracies.

New irritations were not long in following. On February 9 Stalin made a speech that had serious repercussions in Britain and America. On rereading at a distance of twenty years it does not seem so terribly incendiary. In all probability it was made largely to justify the maintenance of a large military establishment, and was not intended as a direct challenge to the West. But it stressed the possibility of a future clash between Communism and capitalism, and its dogmatic tone was certain to arouse much distrust in the United States. Indeed, Mr. Justice Douglas of the Supreme Court described it privately as the declaration of World War III. The answer to this speech of Stalin's came on February 27 from one of the most influential politicians on the Republican side in the Senate of the United States. Arthur Vandenberg of Michigan had been in the Senate since the election of 1928. Originally an isolationist, he had undergone a profound—and undoubtedly a sincere—conversion after Pearl Harbor. President Roosevelt had named him to the American delegation at the conference of San Francisco; he had been very useful there, and had become a firm advocate of the United Nations; he had warmly urged ratification of the Charter; he had accompanied Secretary Byrnes to London at the meeting of the Security Council in January, 1946. While willing to cooperate with the administration, he had become increasingly restive; his interpretation of the Roosevelt diplomacy was highly unfavorable; he believed that the President had conceded far too much at Yalta; he deeply distrusted the Kremlin.

His position is of great significance. For in the events that we are about to describe, the Republicans could best be rallied behind a firm policy. To such a policy the administration itself was becoming more and more disposed; but it is important to note that the pressure of the political opposition operated to intensify the growing antagonism to the Soviet Union. It is always easier (for such is the power of national egotism) for the opposition to advocate a stiff foreign policy than to advocate what is likely to be labeled as appeasement. By his speech of February 27 Senator Vandenberg was contributing to the hardening of American opinion. His words were sure to have a substantial influence. Stressing the fact that two great rival ideologies found themselves face to face, he went on to say, "There is a line beyond which compromise cannot go; even if we have previously crossed that line under the exigencies of war, we cannot cross it again."

The support that came to the Senator from Michigan was not lost upon the administration. The very next night Secretary Byrnes echoed his tone; but far more dramatic was what took place at Fulton, Missouri, on the 8th of March. At this time Winston Churchill was visiting the United States to make an address at Westminster College in Fulton. With the President sitting near him, he launched upon one of the great polemic speeches of which he was a master. Speaking as a private citizen (he had been defeated in the elections of 1945), he aimed his shafts directly at the Soviet Union. Declaring that an iron curtain had descended over eastern Europe, he roundly denounced the concept of the police state; and, stressing the danger of the spread of Communism in western Europe, the former prime minister called for what was virtually an alliance between the United States and Great Britain. With his usual eloquence he asked for joint action in defense of freedom. And in a pointed passage he declared that the secret of the bomb, which belonged to both Great Britain and the United States (since the two nations had collaborated in the investigations that made the bomb possible), must be maintained. We cannot measure the effects of this address with accuracy. But that it played an important part in arousing American opinion is probable.

It is significant, too, that it was answered almost at once by Stalin. "To all intents and purposes," declared the Russian leader, "Churchill now takes his stand among the war-mongers. Mr. Churchill begins to set war loose also by a racial theory, maintaining that only nations speaking the English language are fully pledged, called upon to decide the destinies of the entire world."

There followed another step in the gradual abandonment of quiet discussion in favor of public controversy. At the next Council of Foreign Ministers in April, Secretary Byrnes insisted that discussion should be public. The result, as might have been expected, was to dramatize the differences between the Western powers and the Kremlin, rather than to expedite understanding.

Yet it is important to note that there was as yet no definite breach. Despite a good many arguments and differences of view, it was still possible to provide for the signing of peace treaties with the German satellite states and with Italy in the summer of 1946. It was not Poland, or Rumania, or any other of the eastern states, that presented to the West the insoluble problem. The key to the future relations of Russia and the West lay in the disposition to be made of the German problem.

Before turning to this aspect of the foreign relations of the United States, we should pause to assess American diplomacy as it related to eastern Europe. The story reveals a characteristic weakness, an attempt by moral pressure to exert a decisive influence, where the hard facts of power suggest failure from the outset. The process of the Communization of eastern Europe had by no means been completed by the summer of 1946. But the attempt to arrest it had certainly not succeeded. The compromises made to preserve a democratic façade in Poland, in Rumania, in Bulgaria, had all been no more than the prelude to Russian supremacy.

To say this is not, of course, to say that had the American government frankly recognized the supremacy of the Kremlin in eastern Europe, such action would have paved the way for friendly understanding with Moscow. Nothing is less likely. The outward push of the Soviet Union was not to be arrested so easily. Acquiescence would not have altered the fundamental fact that there existed in 1946 a great competition for influence between Communism on the one hand and the democratic states on the other.

This competition, we have already said, was most significant with regard to Germany. And here interest, as well as ideological considerations, influenced the situation most profoundly. For the Western states, the events of the period following Versailles were still a vivid memory. They pointed to the folly of attempting to exact great reparations from Germany; they suggested the necessity of bringing this energetic nation, with its great resources, into association with the rest of Europe. An impoverished Germany, dependent upon the charity of the victors, could hardly be the object of Western policy. For the Kremlin, on the other hand, Germany was a nation to be plundered; the immense war losses sustained by Russia suggested that the weaker Germany was, the better; and the policy of pushing the Poland boundary westward, and depriving the defeated power of great resources both in population and wealth, was entirely logical. Here again the course of events had followed the power situation; and the objections of the Western powers had been ineffectual in arresting the installation of the new Poland on territories that had long been German.

From these facts there followed a corollary. The Soviet Union could have no objection to dividing Germany; a prostrate Reich was in the Russian interest; cooperation between the Western powers and Moscow in the upbuilding of a new German regime was, from the outset, the most unlikely of possibilities. On this key question, infinitely more important than the question of Poland, or of Rumania, there came a breach that pushed forward the ever-growing rupture between the Kremlin and Washington.

At the outset, compromise was the objective of American diplomacy. Reparations there were to be, despite the lukewarm attitude of the Americans, though Secretary Byrnes stoutly resisted the contention that the total exacted from the defeated power should be in the neighborhood of twenty billions, a figure that Roosevelt, evasive as so often, had mentioned as a basis of discussion. Partial agreement was reached at Potsdam. Each power was to satisfy its claims by the removal of capital equipment in its own zone. Since Germany's industrial power was concentrated in the western part of the country, and food production in the east, the Russians were able to get a quarter of the confiscable plants in the zones occupied by the British and the Americans. In exchange, they were to deliver food and coal to the British and American zones up to 50 per cent of what they got in reparations. The broader question of what was confiscable was dealt with by leaving to the Germans a standard of living that should not exceed the average standard of living in continental Europe.

There were, as the reader will easily see, plenty of holes in this agreement, but it did at least represent an attempt at understanding.

In the same spirit, the American government sought to take account of the Russian fear of a revived and militarized Germany. As early as September, 1945, at the first meeting of the Council of Ministers, Byrnes proposed to Molotov that the four powers, the United States, Great Britain, France and the Soviet Union, should enter into a four-power treaty of guarantee against German agression, the treaty to run for twenty years. It is doubtful whether this proposal was ever transmitted by Molotov to Stalin; if it was not, it was certainly not the first time the Russian foreign minister neglected to inform the dictator of proposals that Molotov did not find to his own liking. But at Moscow in December Byrnes brought up the matter again, addressing himself directly to the Russian autocrat. He appears to have gotten the impression that the Russians might welcome such a step, and at the next meeting of the Council in April he brought forward a formal draft. His proposal, it is needless to say, represented an important departure from the traditional norms of American diplomacy. The results, however, were not encouraging. When Molotov asked that any such engagement run for forty years, instead of twenty, and when Byrnes agreed, new objections were immediately brought forward. In particular the question of reparations was once again raised, and Roosevelt's somewhat casual statement that twenty billion dollars might be taken as a basis of discussion was transformed into a promise that this sum should be definitely fixed, and that half of it should be allotted to the Soviet Union. At the next meeting of the Council in July Molotov brought forward another proposal that could hardly make for understanding, that is, international control of the Ruhr. By this time the possibility of an accord on the German question was virtually out of the question.

It had been made more diffcult by a whole series of events. As early as May 3 General Clay, in command of the American occupation forces, unable to secure from the Russians any accounting with regard to reparations, and, perhaps still more important, unable to persuade the Russians to lower the economic barriers that separated their zone from that of the Western powers, had suspended the deliveries to East Germany provided for in the agreement at Potsdam. In July a bill providing for a substantial loan to Great Britain passed the House of Representatives and became law. To the Kremlin this was confirmation of a close agreement between the two Western powers, all the more so since the debate revealed a considerable suspicion of the motives of the Soviet Union, and since the hints from Moscow that for Russia, too, a loan woud be acceptable, had met with no favorable response.

On this question of a loan to Stalin's regime, there is something more to be said. The question was raised again and again by those who were coming to regret the closer association with Great Britain that was already evident in the summer of 1946. Yet the plain fact is that economic autarchy that was at the basis of the Russian system made agreement with the Kremlin extremely difficult, if not impossible. During the war agreements had been reached by the Western powers for the establishment of a World Bank and of an International Monetary Fund, and these institutions were by 1946 already in operation. They were, indeed, to play an essential role in the regulation of international trade in the future. The Russian government declined to adhere to these agreements. Its action was denounced by Secretary of the Treasury Vinson as making inevitable the separation of the world into two economic blocs. There was, in fact, much force in this point of view. International economic cooperation implied the presentation to these international bodies of candid statements as to their fiscal and development policies. But the secrecy that was characteristic of Russian diplomacy was to be found in the economic sphere. To make a loan without informing oneself of the situation of the prospective debtor was hardly possible; the British had been made, indeed, to divulge their financial situation in detail in connection with the credit arrangement just mentioned; it seems right to say that even had American public opinion been favorable to the transaction, there would have been many obstacles to any agreement with the Soviet Union.

The doubt extends further. It may well be questioned whether the Soviet Union was really interested in an understanding with the West, except, perhaps, if it could have its cake and eat it too. It was probably well content to temporize, while exploiting to the full its position where its writ ran, in

Eastern Germany no less than in Poland and the Balkans; and the elections held in Austria and Hungary made it all too clear that it could not hope for the triumph of Communism in those countries where it was not in control. While there was not yet an open breach, by the fall of 1946 the hopes of an understanding had pretty well vanished.

To return to the German question, the conduct of Molotov in the July session of the Council of Ministers made it clear that a meeting of minds was hardly to be expected. It was at this time that Secretary Byrnes resolved to redeem one of the major errors of President Roosevelt, and to make it clear that the United States had no intention of withdrawing from the European scene. This he did in a speech of the first importance delivered at Stuttgart on September 6, 1946. Declaring that the United States favored the early reestablishment of a German provisional government, he went on, "I want no misunderstanding. We are not withdrawing. We are staying here. As long as there is an occupying army in Germany, American armed forces will be part of that occupation army." With this statement, with this commitment, came the end of any hope that the Kremlin might have entertained that it would be able to work its will in Germany, or in western Europe in general.

Yet the position of the United States was by no means a bellicose one. Two matters underline a contrary view. One was the readiness of the American government to subject the awesome weapon of the atom to international control. Only a little while after the bombs fell on Hiroshima and Nagasaki, the President appointed a commission to make a report on the future of atomic energy. The result was the so-called Lilienthal-Acheson report, which was submitted by Bernard Baruch to the Security Council of the United Nations in June of 1946. This extraordinary document suggested that atomic energy be placed under the control of an international commission, which should alone have the power to regulate the use of that energy

for war-like purposes, and to determine also the possibilities
of the atom for the days of peace. It was stipulated that the
supplies of uranium anywhere in the world would be placed in
the hands of this body. A system of inspection was to guard
against violation of the convention regulating the development
of atomic energy, and as the new system became established,
the United States would hand over to the international authority the atomic weapons in its possession, and these would be
destroyed. In cannot be denied that this was a very far-reaching
proposal indeed, but as we look at the matter over the time perspective of nearly two decades, it is easy to see why it was regarded with no great enthusiasm by the Soviet Union. It left the
United States for an indefinite period in the future in a position
superior to that of any other power; it meant, as a Russian com-
mentator pointed out, that the Soviet Union would give up its
uranium, and trust to the future that the United States would
fulfill its engagements; it involved a violation of that privacy to
which the Russian government was almost pathologically attached; it placed international control of the atom in the hands
of an authority in which the Soviet Union could hardly hope to
exert an influence comparable to that of the Western powers;
and in its provisions for the application of energy to peaceful
purposes it ran counter again to that autarchical spirit that distinguished the Communist society. Taking into account all
these things, it is not strange that the Soviet Union showed little
enthusiasm for this plan, and that it preferred to press for the
destruction of all atomic weapons within a three-months period.
We can be pretty sure today that the Kremlin from the outset
had no other purpose than to procure for itself the weapons that
had been used so dramatically to bring the war to an end.

Yet we must not regard the American proposal as naive. It
sprang from the strain of American thought which has always
desired to see nationalism yield to internationalism, and it certainly aroused strong support in the United States.

Moreover, the legislation that passed Congress in 1946 to

provide for a national commission for the control of atomic energy, after a bitter struggle, placed that control in the hands of civilians, and to all but the cynics, this decision was a signal proof of the peaceful disposition of the United States. Still more important, at the very time when the American government possessed a weapon which no other nation possessed, it did not use its power in any threatening way, and sought, on the contrary, to find a feasible formula for the diminution of its own power.

The failure of the American proposal dramatized what became clearer with time. The position, the interests, and the ideals of the United States and the Soviet Union were opposed to one another; today it seems almost inconceivable that any formula could have been found that would reconcile them. If anything is ever inevitable, the clash of these two powers was inevitable.

Yet it did not seem so to all Americans in 1946. The illusion that reason and good will would solve the problem was one still widely held. In the cabinet this point of view was represented by Henry Wallace, the Secretary of Commerce. As early as March, 1946, he had written a letter to the President expressing the hope that the United States could improve our economic relations with the Soviet Union, and suggesting that "a new group" go to Moscow to discuss the possibilities of economic understanding. Even the most casual reading of this letter suggests who the leader of this "new group" was to be. Very properly, the President paid little heed. Some time earlier, indeed, in January of 1946, he had written to Secretary Byrnes that he was "tired of babying the Soviets." In July in another letter Wallace returned to the charge. But the climax came when in September the secretary addressed a large meeting in Madison Square Garden. Again he advanced the thesis that understanding was possible, and that we ought to keep our hands off Eastern Europe. "The real treaty we need," he said, "is between the United States and Russia. On our part we should recognize

that we have no more business in the political affairs of Eastern
Europe than Russia has in the political affairs of Latin America,
Western Europe and the United States. Whether we like it or
not, the Russians will try to socialize their sphere of influence
just as we try to democratize our sphere of influence. This ap-
plies also to Germany and to Japan. The Russians have no more
business in stirring up native Communists to political activity
in Western Europe, Latin America, and the United States than
we have in interfering with the politics of Eastern Europe and
Russia."

If one reads this speech twenty years after, it does not seem
totally misguided. What Wallace was propounding was a new
doctrine of the balance of power. As a practical matter, moreover, the United States had already conceded to the Soviet
Union much of what he advocated conceding. Byrnes' diplomacy had been pretty ineffectual, and was to be proven more so,
with regard to the region under the aegis of Russian arms.
What was wrong about the speech was the assumption that the
Russians would stay within the zone marked out for them, and
refrain from meddling in other areas. And what was particularly wrong was Wallace's failure to perceive the central nature
of the struggle over Germany. This, indeed, is what most of
those who have written of this period in the spirit of appeasement have not seen. The future of this powerful and competent
nation could hardly fail to be a matter of the first importance
to the United States. Yet by the summer of 1946 the Russians
had made it clear beyond peradventure that they intended to
put every obstacle in the way of German unification under
democratic forms. As Byrnes stated at Stuttgart, the difference
of opinion on this question was irreconcilable.

The Wallace speech kicked up a tremendous furor. Byrnes
protested to the President; Senator Vandenberg, a member of
the American delegation attending with Byrnes a conference in
Paris, issued a public statement declaring that we must know
whether the President was behind the secretary of state, and

adding that we could not have two secretaries at the same time. In the course of the next few days the President demanded Wallace's resignation. The episode illustrates the fact that a coalition was forming behind the President on the basis of a policy of resistance to the Kremlin. On the left there were still those, chiefly among the Democrats, who still talked of appeasement. On the right, chiefly among Republicans, there were still those who were attracted by isolationism, supporting their position by appeals to fiscal solvency and traditional doctrine. But in a very wide center group there was, and was to be, substantial support of the President.

In the closing months of 1946 the situation with regard to Europe, so far as the diplomats were concerned, was one of stalemate. There seems little doubt that the Russians wanted it that way. The economic situation of Europe was distressing. Since dogmatists find little difficulty in believing what they want to believe, it may well be that in the Kremlin the hope of a social collapse in Europe was held more tenaciously than ever. The speeches of Henry Wallace gave encouragement to the idea that a resolute policy would be strongly contested in the United States. The elections to Congress in November turned against the administration. For the first time in sixteen years the Republicans possessed a majority in both houses of Congress. The political reaction, it would appear, was due more to domestic discontent than to lack of support for the administration in the field of foreign policy. But the Kremlin may have believed otherwise.

The relative calm of the close of the year was soon to be broken. We have already indicated that the Kremlin, in retaliation for what it deemed Western interference in its affairs, was taking the offensive. It was putting pressure on the Turks to cede the two important provinces of Kars and Ardaham. It protested strongly the presence of British troops in Greece. This troubled country had been freed of the invader by the British in 1944. In 1946 elections gave a majority to the parties of the right. But guerrilla warfare broke out, particularly virulent along the northern border, abetted, beyond a doubt, by Yugoslavia, Bulgaria, and Albania and certainly not frowned upon by the Kremlin. Matters reached a climax in the winter of 1947. The British government, hard pressed financially, felt compelled in February to notify the United States that it could no longer carry the load, and would withdraw from Greece within a brief period.

It is an interesting question whether the British declaration was intended to force the hand of the United States, or whether the announcement of intention had been preceded by previous correspondence and previous warnings. At the moment, the facts are not clear. What is clear is the decisive manner in which President Truman responded. The British note was delivered on the 27th of February. On the same day the President called in the Congressional leaders and told them that he intended to recommend aid to Greece and Turkey. Congressman Taber, perennial objector, and chairman of the Appropriations Committee in the House, was absent, but those present all concurred. At a second meeting on March 10, with Taber present, all accepted the President's resolve to ask for a Congressional appropriation, and Senator Vandenberg, as always a tower of strength, expressed his strong concurrence. On the 12th Truman appeared before Congress. His specific request was for an appropriation of $400,000,000 for aid to Greece and Turkey. In Greece, he declared, the existence of stable government was threatened by a militant minority, led by Communists. In Turkey, he said, assistance was necessary "for the purpose of effecting that modernization necessary for the maintenance of its national integrity . . . that integrity is essential to the preservation of order in the Middle East." He then proceeded to discuss what he called "the broad implications involved." He stressed the necessity for "the creation of conditions under which we and other nations will be able to work out a way of life free of coercion." He declared it to be "the duty of the United States to support free peoples who are resisting attempted subjugation by armed minorities or by outside pressure." Congress responded by a decisive vote. In the House 160 Democrats and 127 Republicans supported the administration, with 13 Democrats and 93 Republicans opposed. In the Senate 32 Democrats and 35 Republicans voted aye, 7 Democrats and 16 Republicans no.

It is impossible to exaggerate the significance of this legislation. Never before had the eastern Mediterranean been described as an American security interest. Never before had so sweeping a challenge to Communist policy been uttered by a President of the United States. Truman tells us that the original draft declared that the United States *should* support free nations. He changed the word "should" to "must" to make his purpose entirely clear. To describe the Truman speech as epoch-making is not to go beyond the facts.

Those who seek to criticize American policy in the postwar period have from time to time trained their guns on the Truman speech with particular vigor. It came at a time when Secretary Marshall, who had succeded Byrnes at the turn of the year, was in Moscow seeking an understanding with the Soviet Union with regard to the German question. It has been suggested that the President's address was singularly ill-timed, and that it may have prevented some accommodation of Russia and American views on the question of Germany. It has also been suggested that the commitment made was too sweeping, that it would have been better to stick to the specific situation, rather than to lay down such broad principles, which it might or might not be convenient to carry out in practice.

In answer to the first of these criticisms, it ought to be said at the outset that Secretary Marshall knew about, and approved, the projected speech before he left Washington, and that its actual text was cabled to him before delivery. It may also be doubted whether there was, in any case, any real prospect of reconciliation of the views of the Soviet Union and of the United States. At Moscow Molotov again insisted on vast reparations from Germany, and again brought forward the utterly inacceptable suggestion of the internationalization of the Ruhr. It is clear that the Russians preferred a divided Germany to a united Germany that they could not control.

As for the sweeping terms of the Truman speech, broad generalizations have often been in the American technique, from the Farewell Address and the Monroe Doctrine down to Roosevelt's speech on the Four Freedoms. From one point of view, it is true, such generalizations are an imprudence. From another, however, they serve to fire the public mind, which is often ill informed with regard to specifics, but which usually responds to the challenge of idealism. Yet it would be wrong not to recognize the immense significance of the President's language. There is a real question as to how far the national interest of the United States demands interposition in the affairs of regions remote from its own shores, as to how far it is actively, and by military assistance, to extend its responsibilities and its power. The extremist view, in the years ahead, went so far as to talk about "rolling back the iron curtain" and this phrase was heard more than once in the campaign of 1952. The cautious view has sometimes insisted that the United States has been overcommitted. A judgment of this question we shall postpone till later.

For the present let us look back for a moment over the twenty-two month period that had elapsed since the death of Hitler in the bunker in Berlin and the collapse of German resistance. There is always room for the influence of the individual in history, and to call a thing inevitable therefore always involves a certain risk. There are, or at any rate there were then, those who thought that had Roosevelt lived, things might have gone otherwise, and the breach between victors of 1945 have been avoided. Yet the pattern of history, in the large, suggests no such conclusion. Alliances, in their very nature, exhibit centrifugal tendencies when the victory has been won. They also stimulate the nationalistic spirit. In the glow of victory the emphasis changes. Rival dreams of the future supplant the need for cooperation. At the end of the Second World War, the contrast between the Russian dream and the American dream was particularly sharp. There were, it must be conceded, American acts that may have had a part in widening the breach. The rough language with which Truman greeted Molotov on his visit to Washington in April, 1945, the abrupt curtailment of lend-lease, the clear-cut decision to allow no Russian interference in Japan, the challenge to Russian power in eastern Europe and in Iran, all may well have served to convince the Soviet Union of the ill will of the West. But to make these things the *cause* of the Russian position seems to exaggerate their importance. What the Russians held they intended to keep; but their ambitions extended further, and there can be little doubt that they hoped for the collapse of western Europe, and aimed at the domination of Germany.

On the American side, moreover, the drift of opinion is clear. Henry Wallace and his friends continued to agitate in 1947 and 1948, a point to which we may recur. But the pressures on the Truman administration were for a tougher, not a softer, policy. There was an American nationalism as well as a Russian nationalism. Politically, it would have been a risky matter for the Truman administration to sit back and watch the European situation go from bad to worse. It would have been risky on the side of power; it would have been equally risky on the economic side. But to that story I shall refer in another chapter.

I ought not to close this chapter, however, without some further reference to the man who stood at the levers of control during the period we have traversed, and who was to bear the chief responsibility for a further incumbency of six years. Harry S. Truman had been a useful, but hardly a leading, Senator in the years since his election in 1934 until his accession to the vice presidency. His nomination was due more to political expediency and to his contact with Robert Hannegan, the chairman of the Democratic National Committee, than to any outstanding personal merit. Moreover, he came to the presidential office uninformed about many of the questions with which he had to deal. He knew nothing, for example, of the projected atomic bomb. Moreover, he showed no very conspicuous qualities at the outset of his term. As he tells us in his memoirs, he signed the presidential order canceling lend-lease arrangements without reading it. He was careless about allowing Henry Wallace to deliver speeches that ran counter to the views of his secretary of state. He had in no way captured the imagination of the country, and his party suffered defeat in the elections of 1946. But with that election a new era begins. With the year 1947 he broke with Byrnes and chose one of the most respected and greatest Americans as his secretary of state. And Marshall, in his turn, chose an under-secretary who is one of the notable figures of the period, Dean G. Acheson. The relations of these three men in the next two years were as happy as have ever existed between a president and his principal advisers in the field of foreign affairs. The President knew how to benefit by their advice, and he had the courage and resolution to press the course of action that they urged upon him. It has not always been thus in the history of American foreign policy. There have been presidents who left the conduct of great affairs to the Secretary of State; Warren Gamaliel Harding was an example. There have been presidents who sometimes ignored or by-passed the secretary as did Franklin Roosevelt in connection with Cordell Hull. There have not been many who worked so effectively with their secretaries, never relinquishing control, and never failing to heed advice. This is a fact to bear in mind as we pass from the years of the crystallization of policy to the years of realization.

TWO

The Marshall Plan

The events that have unfolded in the last two decades could hardly have occurred had there not been important changes taking place in economic thinking, both in the United States and in Europe. Two changes in particular arrest our attention: the erosion of the idea of balanced budgets, and the creation of a structure of cooperation in the field of international finance.

In the world of theory, the first of these changes will be forever connected with the name of John Maynard Keynes. It is doubtful, however, whether by 1945 the Keynesian views of governmental finance had penetrated very deeply into the American mind. And it is fairly certain that they had not yet become public property in the political domain. It is clear that Roosevelt never understood them. The British economist, when he visited the President in 1934, formed a low opinion (and quite rightly) of his knowledge of economic theory. Nor is it likely that President Truman was instructed in the intricacies of government debt management. Nothing in his previous career suggests that this was so.

As often happens, it was experience, not theory, that changed the course of American thinking. The country had not been wrecked, as the orthodox thinkers predicted, by the deficit financing of the thirties. It had borrowed enormously during the war, and yet had actually carried on the struggle with a rising standard of living. The lamentations of the conservatives were, it is true, heard again and again in the land, and in the halls of Congress. But among the sophisticated the Keynesian ideas were taking root. At Harvard the Keynesian influence became stronger and stronger, in no small part under the influence of Alvin Hansen and Seymour Harris. At M.I.T. a young professor, Paul Samuelson, was propagating the new ideas, declaring that the theory of the British economist was to the economists revelation akin to that experienced by Keats on reading Chapman's *Homer*. The penetration of the new doctrine into the government may be illustrated by the position taken by Marriner Eccles, an influential member, and one-time governor, of the Federal Reserve Board. Among business men the Committee for Economic Development, in which one of the leading spirits was Beardsley S. Ruml, cautiously propounded the incendiary notion that budgets need not necessarily be kept in balance on an annual basis. The spread of these ideas was slow. But the Employment Act of 1946 implicitly accepted the idea of budgetary management and the Council appointed under this act was the source of further Keynesian ideas, particularly through one of its members, Leon Keyserling. By the time of the Eisenhower administration, conservative though it was, the new chairman of the Council, Arthur M. Burns, while sceptical of Keynesianism, was not averse to using budgetary means to cushion the effects of recessions. Today, so highly conservative an economist as Milton Friedman of the University of Chicago has declared that Keynesianism is generally accepted doctrine.

In the long view, Keynesian economics has undoubtedly made easier the programs of foreign aid that have become a normal part of American foreign policy. But considerations of another nature more powerfully influenced the inception of the Marshall plan, considerations having to do with the international monetary system. It is not often that foresight distinguishes the action of democratic governments, but in regard to this problem it did so. At American suggestion, there took place in July, 1944 at Bretton Woods, New Hampshire, a monetary conference of profound significance. It was recognized that in the 1930's monetary disorders had been serious, and had had far-reaching effects. The devaluation of the pound in 1931, the abortive London Economic Conference of 1933, the whimsies of Roosevelt's gold-buying program were unpleasant memories. Was it possible to avoid similar experiences at the end of the war? It was foreseeable that at that time the United States, in view of its immense advances to its allies, would be a creditor nation on a hitherto unprecedented scale. How was Europe to maintain its trade, and carry on the process of recovery, if it lacked dollars to buy the necessary products to start its industry on the upward road? How was monetary order to be preserved in the postwar world?

To a degree Bretton Woods gave an answer. The conference provided for the establishment of an International Bank for Reconstruction and Development, with a capital of 10 billion dollars contributed by the United States. And still more important, there was set up an International Monetary Fund to act as a kind of clearing-house of the various national currencies. The nations subscribing to the Fund (and most of them did so) were to agree not to alter the value of their currencies by more than 10 per cent without the concurrence of the majority. The Fund was supported by contributions from the member countries in gold and in dollars. The creation of these institutions was to be of far-reaching effect, and demonstrated widespread concern about an important problem.

But before the Fund and the Bank had been in operation for any considerable time, signs of distress began to appear in the monetary field. The need of Europe for dollars was patent. Something must be done to meet the immediate situation. The budgetry situation of the United States at that particular juncture was not unfavorable. It could reasonably be hoped, therefore, that Congress would not oppose the necessary measures of financial aid.

The winter of 1946-47 was one of the bitterest that Europe has ever experienced. One result was a food shortage which created a real crisis. Large importations from the United States were necessary to provide for the needs of great elements of the population. Dollar investments abroad had been drained away by the war. The recovery of industry had not proceeded far enough to provide the exports to pay for imports. The British loan had been spent much faster than had been expected, owing to the rise in prices in the United States. Despite the very substantial sums that had been provided by American aid since the end of the war (amounting to over 11 billion dollars), it was clear that much more assistance was required if a serious economic crisis was to be avoided.

There are other factors that help to explain the evolution of the Marshall plan. The humanitarian tradition of the United States is one of them. At the end of the war the American government had taken the initiative in the creation of the United Nations Relief and Rehabilitation Administration, with an American Director-General, Herbert H. Lehman, and a subscription of something over 2 billion dollars. This fund, we should note, was not spent in western Europe. Most of it went to the countries that lie beyond that area, to Greece, to Yugoslavia, to Czechoslovakia, to Poland, and in small amounts (relatively) to Albania, Belorussia and the Ukraine. The list of course suggests, in most instances, that along with the humanitarian motive was a desire to erect a barrier against the spread of Communism. Nor is it possible to deny that in the course of the evolution of the Marshall plan, the fear of social revolution played a very substantial part in the formation of public opinion.

Of the early steps in the State Department itself toward dealing with the situation, we have the account of an insider in Joseph Jones' *Fifteen Weeks.* The initiative, to use Jones' own words, came from Dean Acheson, the under-secretary of state. As early as March 5, 1947, while the Truman Doctrine was under discussion, Acheson wrote to the secretaries of war and of the navy suggesting that the State, War and Navy Coordinating Committee (a committee already in existence) study, in consultation with the Treasury, the larger implications of the international situation. On the 11th, a special committee was appointed to examine the needs of other countries than Greece or Turkey that might require longer-range foreign aid. In the State Department, to work with this committee, a committee on extension of aid to foreign governments was constituted to study especially the financial problems that might be involved. The activities of these committees ought not to be depreciated. Much useful work was done. But movement was much accelerated when, on April 28, Secretary Marshall asked George Kennan to study, as a matter of top priority, the question of aid to Europe. Mr. Kennan had had much experience with the Russians as a member of the embassy in Moscow; he had been recently appointed as chairman of a newly-created body, the Policy Committee, which was instituted to get away from bureaucratic procedures and analyze the fundamentals of policy, and he was given a group of associates well qualified to participate in his task.

While the Kennan committee was carrying on its deliberations, Acheson, with the concurrence of the secretary, launched a trial balloon in a speech at Cleveland, Mississippi. The impact of this speech was not extensive, but it was followed up by more and more contacts with the newspaper correspondents who operated in the State Department. Thus a certain amount of preparation had been made when Secretary Marshall addressed the Harvard Alumni at the Commencement on June 5. Few speeches have had a greater importance. Calling attention to the distress of Europe, he declared that the United States should do whatever it was able to do to "assist in the return of normal economic health in the world, without which there can be no political stability, and no assured peace. Our policy is directed not against any country or doctrine but against hunger, poverty, desperation and chaos. Its purpose should be the revival of a working economy in the world so as to permit the emergence of conditions in which free institutions can exist." In order that the United States should play a helpful role, the secretary went on, "there must be some agreement among the countries of Europe as to the requirements of the situation and the part these countries themselves would take in order to give proper effect to whatever action might be undertaken by our government. . . . It would be neither fitting or efficacious for this government to draw up unilaterally a program designed to place Europe on its feet economically. This is the business of the Europeans. The initiative, I think, must come from Europe. . . . The program should be a joint one, agreed to by a number of, if not all, European nations."

Before describing the effects of the secretary's speech, we ought to call attention to the fact that it drew no such line of doctrine as had the President's address of March 12. The question of Russian participation in the recovery of Europe was discussed in preparing the speech, and the decision was taken to make no exceptions or distinctions between Communist and non-Communist countries. This decision owed a great deal to Kennan. There is little doubt that he was somewhat shocked by the tone of the Truman Doctrine. In him there was little of the ideologist. His view of Russia was cool, clear, and broad. He had no romantic notions that the Russians could be brought to cooperate with the West. But he thought that the sound basis for aid to Europe was economic, and that even if Communism had never existed, the policy that the secretary was to propose was essentially wise. In advocating that Russia be not excluded from the initial proposals, and in answering the secretary's doubts as to the wisdom of including the Kremlin, he argued that to include Russia was to recognize the values that might come from eastern and western European trade between nations that were great producers of raw materials, like the Soviet Union, and nations that were primarily industrial. The Russians, if they came in, might be expected to contribute, as well as to be beneficiaries.

In taking this view, Kennan was undoubtedly wise, though,

as we shall see, there were powerful reasons for Russian abstention. Politically, it would have been impossible to secure the assent of either France or Great Britain to positive action without at least an effort to enlist the Soviet Union. The notion that it was possible to do business with the Kremlin was still widely held. Why not put the Russians on the spot?

Yet it might have been foreseen, as it seems to this author, that the Russian reaction would almost surely be in the negative. By 1947 the Kremlin had already refused adhesion to the agreements negotiated at Bretton Woods. It could not cooperate with the states of the West without revealing economic facts which it was disposed to conceal. Nor was it convinced that the recovery of Europe was in its interest. The notion that the war would be followed by an economic crisis that would pave the way for Communist success was still entertained by those who conducted the affairs of the Soviet Union.

It is worth while, indeed, to pause for a moment at this point to discuss the ideological viewpoint of the Russians with regard to the proposals put forward by the American secretary of state. It was assumed in Moscow that sinister economic motives were involved. It was assumed that the United States could not survive without foreign trade, and that the trade with Europe was particularly vital. It was assumed that American capitalists were preparing for the exploitation of Europe. It was assumed that the great industrial combines were preparing for the conquest of the Continent.

Let us return to the events of June, 1947. The story is that the British foreign secretary, Ernest Bevin, could hardly believe what he heard when the Marshall speech was transmitted across the seas. His first impulse was to wonder if it was really true, and to institute inquiries to find out in Washington. His second thought, more consonant with sound diplomatic practice, was to assume that it was true, and proceed on that basis. The French, too, became deeply interested. On the 13th the French foreign minister invited Bevin to meet with him in

Paris. The meeting was followed by an invitation to the Russian foreign minister to come to Paris for a discussion of the American proposal. On the 27th the three ministers met in the French capital.

It is probable that the only reason the Soviet Union consented to debate the Marshall plan was that it hoped to throw sand in the gears. The tone of the Russian press in the interval between the Harvard speech and the arrival of Molotov in Paris does not suggest a positive view. Nor does the initial position which the minister took when he arrived in the French capital. The essence of the Russian plan was that each nation should make a list of its specific needs, and that the United States on its part should indicate precisely what it was prepared to grant. Such a proposal would have led, obviously, to all kinds of wrangling and jealousies. From the beginning the United States rejected this idea. Yet it is just possible that Molotov never meant it to be accepted, that he merely wished to string out the discussions while Europe's economic difficulties continued. At any rate, there is an interesting anecdote about the break-up of the conference, which we owe to Secretary Acheson (though, of course, he was not present at the meeting). "It seems," so goes the story, "that Molotov has a bump on his forehead which swells when he is under intense emotional strain. The matter was being debated, and Molotov had raised relatively minor questions or objections at various points, when a telegram was handed to him. He turned pale, and the bump on his forehead swelled. After that, his attitude suddenly changed and he became much more harsh. I suspect that Molotov must have thought that the instruction sent to him from Moscow was stupid; in any case the withdrawal of the Russians made operations much more simple."

One wonders if the Russian withdrawal was not hoped for and expected at least by the Secretary and the Under-Secretary. Though the Harvard speech contains no direct appeal to fear of the Kremlin, there are certain phrases with regard to "free nations" which could have no applicability to the Soviet Union. That Marshall had little confidence in the Kremlin goes without saying, after his earlier experience in Moscow in the spring. His suspicions were expressed in the speech on the 5th of June. "Any government which maneuvers to block the recovery of other countries cannot expect help from us. Furthermore, governments, political parties, or groups which seek to perpetuate human misery in order to profit therefrom politically or otherwise will encounter the opposition of the United States." In the same general tone, but more specifically. Acheson on the 15th of June spoke of the Soviet Union in far less conciliatory terms. "In Eastern Europe," he declared, "the Soviet Union, over American and British protests, has used its dominant military position to carry on a unilateral policy, contrary to the Yalta agreements, by which free control of their destiny has been denied these peoples. Even more important, the minority Communist regimes fastened upon these peoples have acted to cut them off economically from the community of Europe, curtail their productivity, and bind them to exclusive relations with the Soviet Union. As a result, the recovery of Europe has been long delayed—tragically."

It was not long before Russian opposition to the Marshall plan became completely clear. On the 3rd of July, Bevin and Bidault addressed a communiqué to twenty-two European nations inviting them to send representatives to Paris to discuss a European recovery plan. Under Russian pressure Poland and Czechoslovakia declined. In the case of Poland, the reason stated was that Germany was to be given more aid than its victims, and that France and Great Britain would occupy a privileged position. In the case of Czechoslovakia events of a more dramatic character took place. The ministry, its Communist members included, first accepted the invitation. Then Gottwald, the premier, and Masaryk, the foreign minister, were haled to Moscow, read the riot act by Stalin himself, and sent back to Prague to draw up a note of declination. This brutal intervention in the affairs of an independent state was accompanied by the negotiation of treaties between the Soviet regime and the satellite states that bound them more firmly than ever to the Russian orbit, and by the establishment of a new organization, the Cominform. The lines were sharply drawn between the East and the West.

Despite Russian opposition sixteen powers met in Paris before the end of July to draw up a program. There was created a European Committee of Economic Cooperation which worked throughout the summer and which, laboring at white heat, presented to the American government on September 22 a detailed analysis calling for four years' economic assistance, and pledging the states concerned to certain broad policies which would facilitate the operation.

The conditions that the OEEC attached to the report ought to claim our particular attenion. For some persons there exists a rather sentimental attitude toward foreign aid, the feeling that with its immense resources the United States can well afford generous assistance to other lands. This feeling is of course creditable to those who experience it, but it does not even scratch the surface of the problem. Forcign aid, as the United States has learned by long experience, is a matter of technique, as well as of compassion and of a perceived interest in world economic growth. Our perspective today, and especially our experience with the Alliance for Progress, underlines the fact that aid to be effective must meet certain general conditions. It was because the report of the OEEC did meet these conditions that it was to become the basis of the most fruitful experiment in international cooperation that has taken place since the war.

The first condition laid down was that of financial stability. The participating powers bound themselves to the maintenance of fiscal responsibility. They forswore inflationary fiscal policies, which might easily have made a mockery of any assistance furnished by the United States.

In the second place, they pledged themselves to cooperation

among themselves in the field of production, in development of trade and resources, and in an effort to bring their international trade into some kind of balance or an approach to balance. In other words, they envisaged the elimination or at least the lowering of customs barriers, and the creation of a genuine European economic order.

In the third place, they gave assurances that an attempt would be made by an expansion of exports to keep the international trade situation within bounds, and to move toward a diminution of dollar deficits.

Fourthly, they promised a strong production effort to restore the position of European agriculture and to advance industrial production.

Finally, they pledged themselves to move toward the stabilization of their currencies.

In the meantime similar efforts to prepare the way for the adoption of the Marshall plan had been made in the United States. What is striking is the extent of participation in these efforts. Indeed, we do not always appreciate the impetus given by the war to widespread collaboration between the government and private interests. Though there was plenty of the old individualistic temper, there was a new spirit that had flowered, and that found impressive expression. As at San Francisco, at the time of the adoption of the Charter of the United Nations, the aid of many influential people was enlisted in preparing the groundwork for the appeal to Congress. A President's Committee on Foreign Aid, headed by Averell Harriman, a former ambassador to the Soviet Union, contained representatives of industry, of labor, of agriculture, of finance, of public administration, and of university administration. This committee analyzed the needs of the European community, and came to the conclusion that over a four-year period a sum of from 12.5 to 17.2 billion dollars would be required. Its report was ready for the President by the first of November, 1947.

At the same time a second committee, under the chairmanship of Secretary of the Interior Julius A. Krug, subjected the economic position of the United States to an exhaustive analysis, in which it was assisted by the recently created Council of Economic Advisers, headed by Edwin G. Nourse. These bodies did not come to identical conclusions, but both of them made it clear that the recovery of Europe was a fundamental American economic interest.

While the Krug and Harriman committees were laboring in the summer of 1947, the Kremlin was, as so often, confirming the American conviction that it intended to dominate eastern Europe, rather than to act in cooperation with the West. In the negotiations of 1946 with regard to the political organization of the states of eastern Europe, the Russians had thrown a sop to the West, promising some recognition of other groups than the Communists. In 1947 they threw off the disguise. In Poland, the elections of January had been marked by outright intimidation of non-Communist groups, and the virtual elimination of the Peasant Party from the government. In October, Mikolaczyk, the leader of that party, and the champion of democratic principles, faced with constant harassment, fled the country. In Rumania, the National Peasant Party under Juliu Maniu was dissolved, and its leader arrested and imprisoned. In Bulgaria the peasant leader, Petkov, was hanged. But the most spectacular evidence of Russian purpose came in Hungary. There in the free elections of the fall of 1945 the Smallholders Party had actually won a majority. But the Communists never ceased to bore from within. With the assistance of the Russian army leaders (Hungary was still under occupation), they managed to make life increasingly difficult for the Hungarian leader, Nagy. They contrived a plot against him, and forced his resignation. While they were not yet strong enough to establish an outright Communist regime, they were obviously in control of the situation and in the elections of August the Communists emerged as the largest single party in the Parliament.

In the United States the key figure to be considered in connection with the Marshall plan was Senator Vandenberg. We have already alluded to his part in the enactment of the bill giving aid to Greece and Turkey, but we need to emphasize more fully than we have yet done the transcendent importance of his role in the fall of 1947 and the winter of 1948. Vandenberg, it must be remembered, had been in the Senate since 1928. With the Republican control of Congress in 1946, he became the chairman of the Committee on Foreign Relations. His knowledge of parliamentary maneuver was extraordinary, his eloquence in presenting his case, though somewhat orotund, was nevertheless impressive, and his conviction with regard to policy was undoubtedly sincere. The fact that he had been an isolationist in the days before Pearl Harbor gave added force to the intensity with which he now advocated active participation in the politics of the world. His experience in association with Byrnes at the conferences with the Russians, at London in the winter of 1946, and at Paris when the peace treaties with the satellites were signed, had confirmed him in the clear conviction that the times called for a positive policy and for a check to Russian ambition. Men called him vain, and vain he undoubtedly was. But it matters little. This is neither the first, as it will not be the last, time at which egotism has been placed at the service of the public good.

There was much potential opposition to Vandenberg on his own side of the party aisle. There was, for example, Senator Wherry of Nebraska, the Republican whip, who, before his entry into politics, had been an undertaker and whose allegiance to dead ideas was very appropriately substantial. Far more important was Senator Taft of Ohio. A man of very real abilities, standing head and shoulders above the rank and file on the Republican side, he was an intense partisan. He frequently expressed his conviction that the business of an opposition was to oppose. He might have made things very difficult indeed. But apart from Vandenberg's skill in handling men, a very substantial asset, there was another factor that entered into the account, and disarmed Taft as the resolute leader of the opposition. His very partisanship made him reluctant to accentuate a party division, and his ambitions for the presidency, one might suspect, operated in the same direction. At any rate, he was less troublesome than he might have been. Reading his many speeches, one would often think that he was almost irreconcilable, a politician of the *Chicago Tribune* school. But when it came to action, the record looks different. Though he did not go the whole way, it is remarkable how far he did go. His unwillingness to challenge Vandenberg was one of the important factors in the eventual acceptance of the Marshall plan.

There is more to be said with regard to Vandenberg. The constructive attitude taken by the administration owed a great deal to him. The preparation of the submission of the Marshall plan to Congress was due, at least in part, to his suggestions. By raising objections, by insisting on careful study, by cajoling his friends on the Republican side, he played a vital role in the events of the fall of 1947. After the passage of the Greco-Turkish aid bill in March, the Senator had assured his colleagues that no more funds for foreign nations would be asked for that year. But when the autumn came around, he managed to extricate himself from this promise, and played a part, as we shall see, in the enactment of the interim aid legislation which passed Congress toward the end of the year. It was partly due to him that the House, which was less easy to convince than the Senate, appointed a special committee to study the problem, under Christian A. Herter, a representative from Massachusetts. The committee visited Europe, and came back firmly convinced that the situation called for positive action.

But the dominant explanation of the events we are about to analyze was undoubtedly the trend of public opinion. We have already seen that the Kremlin did its bit in this regard. By the end of 1947 Truman felt able to call Congress in special session, not to enact the Marshall plan in its entirety (that would have to wait for the next session of Congress), but to provide stopgap aid for Austria, France, and Italy. The debates that took place toward the end of the year gave extraordinary evidence of the depth of public sentiment. In the Senate Vandenberg provided brilliant leadership. In the House the Republican leaders took the affirmative, not the negative, point of view. When the time came for a vote, the House passed the stopgap or interim aid bill without a roll call. In the Senate the final vote was 83 to 7, with most of the senators on the Republican side joining their Democratic colleagues.

With the winter there came a systematic organization of public feeling such as has rarely occurred when a question of foreign policy was under debate. In October Henry L. Stimson, former secretary of war and secretary of state, wrote an article in *Foreign Affairs* that boldly called for a world role for the United States and for recognition of the fact that the United States had become "for better or worse" a wholly committed member of the world community. At the turn of the year a Committee for the Marshall Plan was formed, and Stimson became its national chairman. An executive committee was constituted with representatives of every aspect of American life. Three hundred prominent citizens from all parts of the country accepted membership. Funds were collected, advertisements were inserted in the newspapers, and the support of many other agencies was invited. Church groups, labor groups, farm groups, business groups (in this last category the Chamber of Commerce of the United States was most notable) took part in the great popular movement to support the Marshall proposal.

It is not to be supposed, of course, that all this support was disinterested. The Marshall plan appealed to the shipping interests on obvious grounds. The international financial community was naturally favorable. Farming interests, at least some of them, saw in the proposal an opportunity to dispose of their products. But with all this there was much genuine idealism, much of the kind of feeling that led Winston Churchill later to describe the Marshall Plan as "the most unsordid act" in history.

The legislative history of the Marshall Plan we can describe only briefly. Public hearings began almost at once with the convening of the new session of Congress in January. Debate in the Senate was opened by Senator Vandenberg on March 1.

His speech on that occasion merits quotation. "Within the purview of this plan," said the senator, "are 270,000,000 people of the stock which has largely made America. They are 26% of all the literates of the earth. Before the war they operated 68% of the ships that sailed the sea. They produced 27% of the world's cereals. They produced 37% of the world's steel. They sold 27% of the world's exports and bought 39% of the world's imports. They are struggling, against great and ominous odds, to regain their feet. They must not be allowed to fail. The world —America emphatically included—needs them as both producers and consumers. Peace needs their healthy restoration for the continuing defense of those ideas by which free men live. This vast friendly segment of the world must not collapse. The iron curtain must not come to the rim of the Atlantic either by aggression or by default. This is a plan for peace, stability and freedom. As such it involves the self-interest of the United States. It can be the turning point in history for 100 years to come. If it fails, we will have done our final best. If it succeeds, our children and our children's children will call us blessed. May God grant his benediction upon the ultimate event!"

As in the preceding September, Vandenberg's tactical sense served him well. To meet partisan suspicions that the political benefits of the plan would redound to the interests of the Truman administration, it was decided that the plan would be administered by a new agency, independent of, but acting in cooperation with, the Department of State. To meet the objections to recommendations of the committees that drafted the proposal for a sum of $17 billion over a period of four years, it was agreed that Congress should retain its annual control over appropriations and that the initial sum appropriated should be for only twelve months. In a most ingenious expedient, it was provided that each European government should deposit in a special fund (a so-called counterpart fund) a sum equal to that which it received from the United States. Ninety-five per cent of this was to be used to promote recovery; the other 5 per cent was to be spent in meeting the costs of administration. Some concessions were made to special interests; 50 per cent of all goods shipped abroad under the assistance plan were to be shipped in American vessels; to satisfy the milling interests it was provided that 25 per cent of all wheat sent abroad was to be in the form of flour. Thus were specific economic groups brought to the support of the legislation.

There was little doubt from the time the debate began that the bill would pass. But the Soviet Union, as so often, contributed effectively to the result. In February, with Soviet support and at Soviet instigation, the Communist elements in the government of Czechoslovakia displaced most of the other elements in the cabinet and set up a totalitarian regime. In Italy, the Communist party, in the midst of the spring elections, did everything it could to oppose the plan, and thereby stimulated American efforts to emphasize its benefits, and thus to assure a victory for the Christian Democrats. The issue was sharply drawn between the Soviet Union and the West when the bill came to passage. It passed the House of Representatives by a vote of 317 to 84. In the Senate there was not even a roll call. This fact is eloquent testimony of the drift of public opinion. No senator, apparently, wished to reveal his opposition to the measure.

But the struggle was not yet over. The measure with which we have been dealing was merely an *authorization* bill. The actual appropriation of funds had to come later. This, too, was to pass by majorities about as large as those of the previous enactment. But before the vote came, there occurred a parliamentary episode that is so revealing of the structure of American government and of the political game as it is played in the United States that it deserves to be fully described.

In the House of Representatives the chairman of the appropriations committee was a hard-boiled representative from Auburn, New York, John Taber, who had deservedly won the name of "Meatax John." A bitter foe of public expenditure, he succeeded in getting his committee to cut drastically the appropriation for the Marshall plan, though the authorization bill had already been passed endorsing the sum requested, 5.3 billion dollars. He then proceeded to ram his bill through in a Congressional debate that lasted a single day. An amendment introduced by Dirksen of Illinois, later one of the most influential members of the Senate, was defeated on a standing vote without a roll call. Evidently the opponents of the bill did not wish to be known. When the Democratic ranking member of the Appropriations Committee made a motion to recommit, in the hope of increasing the sums voted, he could not get a second vote of any kind. The bill then was passed in its mutilated form.

Essentially, by their tactics, the Republican leaders, Martin of Massachusetts and Halleck of Indiana, were attempting to conceal the division in their ranks, since the country was on the eve of the Republican nominating convention. But this attempt to paper over the rift in the party's ranks reckoned without Senator Vandenberg. It was almost unprecedented for a Senator to demand to be heard by a House Committee, and indeed Vandenberg at an earlier date had given some reason to believe that he would not interfere with the House action. Now, however, he demanded to present his views in open session. On June 9 he appeared before the committee in one of the most dramatic and courageous acts of his career. His object was not to reverse the House action; indeed the bill had already been passed. It was to strengthen the position of the Senate when the bill went to conference. But Taber was hard to move. The conference lasted five days, even though by this time all the leading candidates for the Republican nomination for the presidency had endorsed the larger figure. In the final event the House was forced to yield. Senator Taft, this time on the side of the angels, announced that he was willing to hold Congress in session indefinitely unless the Senate position on the bill was accepted. At last the recalcitrant Congressman yielded and the larger sum voted by the Senate was accepted. In addition to his appearance before the House Committee, Vandenberg demanded a roll-call vote in the Senate on sending the bill to conference in its more generous form. Only ten Republicans voted against him, and among his supporters were Taft, who in general was quite conservative on this type of issue, and Wherry of Nebraska, who, as we have said, represented in general the very essence of mid-Western isolationism.

Once the struggle was over, the rest was easy. The House accepted the Senate figure and approved the conference report by a vote of 318 to 62. Republicans voted three to one in its favor. In the Senate there was not even a roll call. The bill was signed by the President on June 28.

Before we analyze the effects of the Marshall plan, which were far-reaching, we should mention two respects in which the plan did not fulfill the hopes of its sponsors. The aid to be given under the plan, as has been made clear, was intended to be devoted to economic recovery. But the development of events in Europe made it impossible to follow out this plan. Suffice it to say here that the necessity for rearmament on a substantial scale and the outbreak of the Korean war made it necessary to devote larger and larger sums to military purposes. The appropriations for 1948-49 amounted to a little over $6 billion, all for economic recovery. In 1949-50 the figure was $4.48 billion, with $.7 billion for defense assistance. For 1950-51 the figure was $2.31 billion for economic purposes and $4.96 billion for military ends. In 1952 the respective amounts were $1.62 billion and $4.92 billions. The total figure for economic aid amounted to approximately $13.6 billion.

The second respect in which the Marshall plan disappointed the hopes of its most ardent advocates had to do with the balance of payments, with the dollar shortage that the plan was intended to alleviate. Despite the recovery program, it proved quite impossible for Europeans to develop their foreign trade to the point at which it was brought into balance with that of the United States. The result was the rash of currency devaluations that broke out in Europe in 1949, initiated by the British action in reducing the pound from $4.03 to about $2.80. British action was followed by adjustments by most of the other nations of western Europe. We should be clear as to what this means. By these sweeping devaluations the American market was opened to European imports on an increasing scale. Both the psychological and the practical effects of such a move deserve to be emphasized. They have not commonly been rated at their real value in the diplomatic histories.

These facts, however, do not diminish the immense significance of the Marshall plan itself. Its ramifications were enormous. Perhaps no other enterprise in the field of common economic effort has ever had wider effects.

The student of international affairs may be staggered at its cost. In the four years from 1948 to 1951 the sum spent to stimulate European recovery was something over 13 billion dollars. This seems stupendous. But the gross national product of the United States in 1948, the first year of ERP (as it came to be called), was $213 billion. For the four years 1948 to 1951 it was $1,200 billion. In other words, little more than one per cent of the production of the American people was diverted to foreign economic aid. Nor is this all; the dollars so spent were for the most part spent in the United States. They served to stimulate the American economy as well as to revive the economy of the Old World.

There has probably never been an American public policy that enlisted wider and more enthusiastic support than the Marshall plan. We have already alluded to the wide support given to the legislation itself. The head of the new agency when it came into operation was Paul G. Hoffman, at that time president of the Studebaker Corporation—a dedicated man, highly efficient, and adept in personal relations. His leadership was one of the most important factors in the success of the whole operation. The fact that he was a Republican protected the very large operations of his office from partisan sniping. His ability to select lieutenants was of the first order. As an example of efficient government action the Marshall plan is outstanding.

To turn from the effects of the Marshall plan at home to its effects abroad, the recovery that took place in Europe in the period between 1948 and 1951 was extraordinary from any point of view. It is true that as one contemplates the figures one must take account of the fact that even before the American aid the position was better than one might assume. In 1948, for example, industrial production was already at over 95 per cent of the last peace year, 1938, and agricultural production was at 86 per cent. But the figures for 1951 were 132 per cent on the industrial side, and 114 per cent on the agricultural side. In certain lines of activity the advance was still more striking. Electric power advanced from an index of 144, based on 1938 as 100, to 197. The index number for motor vehicles produced rose from 77 to 181. Steel advanced from 81 to 133. The production of sugar increased from 78 to 153, and of bread from 62 to 104. Part of this increase was due to technological advance, and here American assistance and advice was certainly an important factor. But a large part was due to the energy that the plan generated, and to the hopes it aroused.

In the same way, we must recognize the role of the European governments. Had not an earnest effort been made to bring European budgets under control, and to stimulate exchanges within the European community, the results would have been far less sensational. We ought not to attribute to the United States the sole merit for the Marshall plan. The collaboration which we received from Europe, both in the field of government and in the field of industry, was a vital factor in the success attained.

Of course the Soviet Union did all it could to discredit the policy of the United States. In the view of the Moscow propaganda machine, the Marshall plan was "an instrument of preparation for war," "a means for the economic and political enslavement of Europe," and a means of saving the American economy from postwar collapse. Nor is it to be supposed that this agitation had no effect. There were plenty of Europeans who took a cynical view of the American government's purposes. In particular, French commentary on the plan was frequently tinged with suspicion and with nationalism. But the broad picture is otherwise. The general impression presented to Europe was a fortunate one.

The Marshall plan, however, can never be rightly judged unless it is seen in a very broad perspective. That it contributed to the economic rehabilitation of Europe goes without saying, and hardly needs to be argued. It is with regard to the large question of European unity that it is even more important. Let us examine this matter in some detail.

First of all, and the fact has been insufficiently stressed in the preceding pages, the plan tied Germany firmly to western Europe. The Germans were permitted to take part in the preliminary conversations; they shared in the result. Putting it another way, only a little more than three years after the end of the war, the nation that had been vanquished in 1945 was admitted once again into the European family. No greater act of reconciliation has ever taken place, to my knowledge, in the field of international politics. It is true that the pressure exerted from the East, the folly and selfishness of the Soviet Union, contributed not a little to this result. But even when this is taken into account, it is a remarkable fact that the most disastrous war in the history of Europe ended with an impetus toward European unity. For the stimulus which American policy afforded in this enterprise, the administration of Harry Truman deserves and will assuredly receive from the historian immense credit.

It is not irrelevant, indeed, in connection with the Marshall plan, to sketch briefly the broad movement looking to the closer association of the European states with one another. The picture, it should be said at the outset, is not a simple one, and the results achieved hardly can be said to correspond with the American dream. Americans, in international affairs, are apt to believe that what is good for them must necessarily be good for others. There was therefore after the war a hope that Europe might form a great confederation of states, much as the thirteen American colonies formed a confederation under the stress of the revolutionary war. For a little while, it seemed as if events might move in that direction. Shortly after the inception of the Marshall plan, ten states joined in signing the Statute of London. These states were the three Scandinavian countries, the three Benelux countries, Britain, France, Italy, and Ireland. Later six other countries were added, West Germany, Iceland, Greece, Turkey, Austria, and Cyprus. An ambitious plan of organization was developed. There was to be a consultative assembly, with representation on a population basis. Delegates to the assembly were to be selected by the parliaments of each country, and were to be representative of all political parties. They were to be seated alphabetically, without regard to national origins. Their powers were not great, but they might consider almost any question of international import. There was also to be a secretariat, and a committee of ministers composed of the foreign ministers of each member state. Here indeed in miniature was the germ of a true confederation.

The Council of Europe exists today. Though it has not played a decisive role in the international politics of the last decade and a half, it has been a useful place of contact for the representatives of the states converned, and a clearing-house of ideas. Its importance should not be unduly depreciated. But there have been many reasons why the supranational idea that the Council represented has not in practice developed to meet the hopes of its sponsors. The Scandinavian states, with a long tradition of noninvolvement, feared too close an association with the rest of Europe. Austria, under four-power occupation, had to tread with caution. Turkey was hardly a European power in the ordinary sense of the term. More important than these considerations was the attitude of Britain. In the fifteen years since the war the British position toward Europe has been consistently ambivalent. Powerful forces suggest a closer association with the Continent; on the other hand forces equally powerful have operated in the contrary direction. In 1949 the Labor party was in power. Its interest in national planning and in the planned economy made it leery of committing itself to supergovernmental ideas. At the same time the Tories in Britain had their own reasons for taking the same position. Traditionally attached to the idea of empire, with important commercial associations with the former colonies, and tinged with the nationalism that goes with conservatism in general, they could not divest themselves of their past. Finally, the precarious situation of British finances, illustrated by a series of crises, the devaluation of 1949 among them, suggested caution in going very far along the road of federation.

More positive steps toward the collaboration of European states have been taken since 1945, and some of them, it ought to be said, bear a very definite relationship to the Marshall plan itself. We have already pointed out that the plan involved a decision on the part of the participating states to draw up a program for all of them taken together, instead of each state's formulating its own requirements. The agency instituted for this purpose was the Office for European Cooperation. It continued to exist after its initial purpose had been served. It is virtually an all-European agency, and it includes Great Britain. In 1961 the United States joined this group, and a Development Assistance Committee was formed to coordinate free-world aid and programs for the underdeveloped countries, and to stimulate cooperation among the strong nations of the world for the assistance of the weaker. While the OEEC, as it is now dubbed, has no large authority, it serves as a very useful forum of discussion of economic topics of general interest, and as a means of contact between technical experts of all kinds.

The OEEC devised another agency which, though it has been supplanted, performed, and under a new name still performs, a useful role. This was the European Payments Union, instituted in 1950. The union provided a means for the settlement of trade balances between European countries on a multilateral basis. Hitherto a bilateral system of trade balances had existed, which was cumbrous and complicated. The EPU represented, therefore, a considerable step forward.

Along with these measures of general import were others which, though not directly related in any way to the Marshall plan, illustrate the new tendencies toward economic cooperation in Europe—though on a more restricted basis. The earliest of these in point of time was the Schumann plan, which came into operation in 1950 and which established the European Coal and Steel Community with six members, France, Germany, the Benelux states, and Italy. This provided for common prices for coal, iron, and steel, for the abolition of customs duties on these products, for the free movement of labor in the industry, and even for a new social agency to concern itself with housing, health, and other welfare measures.

The Community was virtually, within its own area, a supergovernment. There was an executive body, known as the High Authority, with nine representatives, two each from France, Germany, and Italy, and one from each of the Benelux countries, whose members were to be chosen by the cooperating governments. This body was given the power to conduct its own finances, through taxation levied on the private enterprises that comprised the Community. It was also given the power of control over these enterprises. There was also a Council of Ministers, whose members were chosen by the respective governments, whose powers were largely consultative. There was a Common Assembly, authorized to review the work of the

Authority and by a two-thirds vote to make changes in the management. The members of this Assembly, though chosen by the governments, did not vote along national lines. Finally, there was a Court of Justice to interpret the treaty creating the Community, and whose decisions were binding on all the members of the Community.

It has sometimes been asked whether this ambitious arrangement in its extraordinarily supranational character might, by the fact that it was restricted to only six nations, actually stand in the way of further integration. Time will answer this question. But, whatever the answer, the striking thing about the Community is the integration of German and French interests to a remarkable degree. By this means German economic interests were firmly tied to the West, the association of French and Germans became closer, and the possibilities of armed conflict between the two nations in the future became remote indeed. The rapprochment between Paris and Bonn is not yet perfect and probably will not be for a long time to come; but none the less a giant stride had been taken toward the extinction of an old and traditional enmity.

Indeed, the Community, established in 1953, was followed by the Treaty of Rome in 1957, in which the six powers of the Community created two new international institutions, the European Atomic Energy Commission and the Common Market.

The Atomic Energy Commission was to become an agency for the exchange of information on scientific and economic questions relating to the development of atomic power. Above the Executive Authority was the Council of Ministers, and the Assembly and Court of Justice created under the Schumann Plan were given appropriate authority in this new field of activity.

The European Common Market envisaged the step-by-step development of a tight customs union and of complete free trade between the members. The process was to be a gradual one. Duties were to be progressively reduced at least 60 per cent by 1966, and completely abolished by 1970. There were ambitious plans for the free movement of goods and commodities, of capital investments, and of labor. There was to be a Council of Ministers, whose decisions, however, would have to be unanimous down to 1970.

The Common Market has had its difficulties, especially since the advent of General de Gaulle, whose enthusiasm for supranational institutions is, to say the least, limited. But none the less substantial progress has been made, and it is safe to predict that more progress will follow.

There is, of course, another side to the whole question of the Common Market. The British, for the same reasons that made them leery of a federated Europe, stood aloof from the movement. The British economy had something to lose, as well as much to gain, by virtual free trade with a large part of the Continent. In particular, membership in the Common Market would complicate her relations with the Commonwealth countries. As a result, Britain constructed a competing organization, the European Free Trade Assembly, composed of Britain, Sweden, Norway, Denmark, Austria, Switzerland, and Portugal. This organization aimed to reduce tariffs on industrial goods, but not on agricultural products. Its organization was much looser than that of the Common Market, and its effectiveness much less. Nor does there seem any possibility at the moment that the two agencies, ECC and EFTA, can be united. The economic unity of Europe is therefore very far from complete. The observer of the present situation can only speculate as to whether the Common Market countries will become a sort of closed economic bloc, or whether the two existing units, the Common Market and the EFTA, will in time merge, or whether some middle course will be devised which will at least bring Great Britain into association with the major states of the Continent. On this latter question, the French attitude has been little less than capricious; and the British, on their part, have not overcome their hesitations and traditions.

What has the United States to say with regard to this whole problem? While there are some inconsistencies in the record, American administrations in general have warmly welcomed the movement toward the economic integration of Europe. When the Office of European Economic Cooperation was set up in 1949, Paul Hoffman made an important speech looking toward the future. He pointed out that the task before the Commission would not be meaningful "unless we have come to grips with our second task—the building of an expanding economy in Western Europe through economic integration. The substance of such integration would be the formation of a larger single market within which quantitative restrictions upon the movement of goods, monetary barriers and the flow of payments and, eventually, all tariffs are permanently swept away." This was more, he went on to say, than an ideal. It meant the creation of a single market of 200,000,000 consumers, and new prosperity in Europe. Even before Hoffman's speech, the United States had participated in the drafting of the General Agreement on Tariffs and Trade, which offered a way to the reduction of tariff duties on the part of this country and of many others. A certain amount of effective work has been accomplished by this organization. And in 1962 Congress gave to President Kennedy wide powers to enter into negotiations for the further reduction of duties. Positive action has been delayed by the controversies among the Europeans themselves. But the atmosphere is perhaps more hopeful today than it has been in many years.

In concluding this chapter it can be said that American economic foreign policy has been, on the whole, extremely enlightened. Cynics will, of course, say that it has been guided by self-interest, and while no well-rounded view of the matter will neglect the element of idealism, and the dream of a united

Europe which lay behind it, neither will anyone deny that American interests have been well served by the policies we have been examining. The heart of the question lies in the fact that the self-interest involved was an *enlightened* self-interest. It is sheer romanticism to imagine that the intercourse of nations will be dictated by sentimentality or altruism. The best that we have a right to hope for, and perhaps to demand, is that the American government will take a broad and not a narrow view of its problems, and that in seeking its own interests, it will serve in substantial degree the interests of the world society. There is a good case for the argument that, by and large, this is precisely what it has done.

THREE

The North Atlantic Pact

In the involvement of the United States in Europe the first step, as we have seen, was the Truman Doctrine. The second was the Marshall plan. The third, of which this chapter treats, was the North Atlantic Treaty. For the first time in its history, the American government entered into a peace-time alliance, committing it explicitly to the use of armed force. President Truman's declaration involved, as we have seen, military aid to Greece and Turkey; and it expressed a vague if broad commitment with regard to the defense of nations threatened by Communism. It was, as we have noted, a very substantial departure from the American past. But it was *not* an alliance. The decision to enter an alliance lay ahead.

There is, however, an historical background to the Atlantic pact which deserves to be considered. In the nineteenth century the doctrine of isolation from the affairs of the Old World remained intact. Even political participation in European questions was eschewed. It was not until 1905 that the United States participated in any European gathering that was concerned with major political problems, and when the Roosevelt administration signed the act of Algeçiras, regulating the status of Morocco, the Senate of the United States, in ratifying the treaty, appended a reservation declaring that its consent implied no departure from the American policy of no entangling alliances. With the First World War the emphasis was still on neutrality, the entrance of the United States into the struggle was brought about not because of any strategic interest, but

by German defiance of the rules of international law governing
the use of the submarine. Had the Germans not committed
the folly of challenging the United States on this issue, it is
difficult to see how the Wilson administration could have been
drawn into the struggle, especially in view of the President's
reelection in 1916 based on the plea that he had kept us out
of war.

Enter the war, however, we did. Yet the American government contracted no alliance with the European nations with
which it was aligned; these, in the President's words, were
associates, not allies. Nor did the President envisage the consolidation, at the end of the war, of the relationship then
formed. On the contrary, he dreamed of an association of *all*
nations, which should, by common action, coerce any aggressor,
and compel him to desist from aggression. This is the key
concept of the League of Nations. We shall have more to say
of this general concept in a later chapter. But two points should
be made here. Fundamentally, the people of the United States
were not ready for any such commitment. The words "League
of Nations" no doubt exercised a certain spell on the American
mind. But when it came down to cases, there was much resistance to any commitment that would bind the United States
to take action against an aggressor. The superficial view of the
fight over the treaty of Versailles regards this struggle as a
partisan contest. There is a substratum of truth behind this
judgment. And as one who felt deeply on the League issue in
1919 and 1920, I must confess that my own views were colored
by this feeling. But a longer view, matured over the years,
has convinced me that American opinion, while in favor of a
League, was by no means prepared to accept a binding commitment of the kind that the President desired. It was possible,
without too great public protest, for the Harding administration
to shelve the whole project. It was possible for as high-minded a
man as Charles Evans Hughes, a supporter of the general idea

of a League, to acquiesce as secretary of state in the decision not to press for ratification of the treaty of Versailles.

Nor does the history of the League suggest that the Wilsonian formula was sound. It may be argued that everything would have been different if the Senate had ratified the treaty. But our subsequent history, the caginess with which Franklin Roosevelt kept away from the League issue in 1932, the caution of the two secretaries of State, Stimson and Hull, in their relations with the Geneva institution, suggests the contrary. Let us not, in any case, attempt to rewrite history by hypothesis.

We cannot, however, leave the question of the League here. The Wilsonian concept, I believe, had a substantial impact on the American mind. It was based on a moral antagonism to aggressive war. And this antagonism certainly played some part in the formation of opinion in the nineteen-thirties.

None the less, the notion of noninvolvement attained great strength in this same period, and was responsible for the so-called neutrality legislation of the thirties, based upon the hypothesis that we could, if we did certain things, and abstained from doing certain other things, keep out of trouble. Matters did not work out that way. The aggressions of Adolf Hitler in the years 1939 to 1941 outraged American sentiment; but what was more, they suggested that there existed a danger to American security. And Japan's attempted conquest of China produced a powerful reaction in the United States. The end result was Pearl Harbor, and American participation in the Second World War. And this time there was an alliance. By the treaty of Washington of January 1, 1942, the war-making powers bound themselves not to conclude a separate peace with the aggressor.

Yet when the war ended, the first thought of American statesmanship was to revive the Wilsonian ideal. The result was the conference of San Francisco and the Charter of the United Nations. The idea of collective security was revived. And this time the Senate acted affirmatively by a crashing vote in the ratification of the new instrument of peace. Not an alliance, but a new coalition of all nations for the maintenance of international tranquility, was what was aimed at in San Francisco in 1945, as in Paris in 1919.

It did not take long, however, for the statesmen of the period to see that this formula was not enough. Indeed, in the drafting of the Covenant, provision was made that for action against an aggressor, the great powers, including Russia, must be in agreement. As a weapon against the Soviet Union, then, the Charter was from the beginning of very doubtful value.

The perception of the limited value of the Charter led the United States in 1947 to negotiate with the states of Latin America a convention calling for common action against an aggressor. This convention, ratified without difficulty by the Senate, though not committing each nation to the use of force, was in fact a kind of alliance, a momentous departure from the precedents, a foreshadowing of what was to come. We shall revert to it in discussing American relations with Latin America.

In Europe, too, however, things were beginning to stir. The aggressive tone of Soviet diplomacy produced its inevitable effect. As early as January 22, 1948, in a speech that was not free from ambiguities, but that clearly expressed malaise at the growth of Soviet power, Ernest Bevin, the British foreign secretary, spoke out for a consolidation of western Europe. More important, in March, five Western nations, France, Great Britain, the Netherlands, Belgium, and Luxemburg, united in a treaty pledging themselves to afford "all military and other aid and assistance in their power" to any one of them that might be the object of an armed attack in Europe. In a sense, this was no more than a gesture. The armed forces of which the signatories disposed were certainly not large enough to resist a Russian invasion of western Europe if one were undertaken. In a very real sense, the treaty of Brussels was intended to be the prelude to an understanding with the United States.

In an address to Congress on March 17, the very day the treaty was signed, President Truman alluded to the great significance of the treaty of Brussels, and expressed confidence that the United States would, "by appropriate means, extend to the free nations the support which the situation requires." But the signing of an alliance with the states of the Old World was too revolutionary a step to be undertaken lightly, or without the full support of the Congress. It was Senator Vandenberg who, as so often, provided the catalyst for the breach with the past. He acted, of course, in close collaboration with the State Department, through the under-secretary, Robert A. Lovett. There were also consultations with Marshall, and with the top Congressional leaders. The result was a resolution drafted by the Senator on May 11 and presented to the Senate on May 19. As we read this document in the light of the present, it seems a most ingenious affair. For the most part it dealt with the means of improving the Charter of the United Nations. With a shrewd political instinct, Vandenberg had based his action on the widespread support of the Charter in the United States. Under cover of this support, and with the declared view of making armed force unnecessary "except in the common interest," the resolution called for "the progressive development of regional and other collective arrangements for individual and collective self-defense in accordance with the purposes, principles and provisions of the Charter" and for "association of the United States by constitutional processes with such regional and other collective arrangements as are based upon continuous and effective self-help and mutual aid, and as affect its national security." After substantial discussion the resolution was passed by the Senate by a vote of 64 to 6. An amendment offered by Senator Pepper of Florida to strike from the resolution all reference to the possibility of military aid was rejected by a vote of 61 to 6. The date was June 11.

The Vandenberg resolution marked a sweeping departure from American diplomatic tradition; it suggested and was aimed at a direct commitment to abandonment of the precedents of a hundred and fifty years. One wonders whether all the senators who voted for it were aware of its far-reaching implications. However this may be, the Kremlin did all that it could in the months that followed to persuade the American people that the projected commitments were necessary. Indeed, there is a sort of fatality about the regularity with which the Soviet Union galvanized American opinion in pursuit of policies which it had every interest in preventing.

The occasion for these new incitements to positive action was to be found in the situation in Berlin. At the end of the war Berlin was placed under four-power control. It was, of course, within the Russian zone, and by an oversight that was later regretted, no written agreement was made ensuring free communication by rail and road with the West. However, an agreement was signed permitting access by air—providentially, as future events were to demonstrate. For a time the four powers, though at odds, operated without extreme friction. But as the general relations of Russia with the Western powers deteriorated so, too, did the situation in Berlin. The passage of the Marshall plan, and above all, the inclusion of Germany in the plan, naturally displeased the Kremlin. By 1948 the British, French and Americans had agreed upon merging the three zones which they controlled, and preparations were under way for the election of a West German government. In the spring of 1948 arrangements were concluded for the institution of a new German currency, and this new currency was also introduced in limited quantities in West Berlin. For some time the situation in the former German capital had been deteriorating, and the Russians had already begun in various ways to put obstacles in the way of traffic with the West. The currency reform appears to have been the last straw. On the 24th of June, 1948, all freight traffic to Berlin through the Russian zone was suspended and electric power generated in East Berlin was shut off from the Western zone. A serious international crisis was imminent.

In the events that followed, the striking thing is the spirit shown by the Berliners themselves. Precariously situated as they were, they made it perfectly clear that they intended to do their full part in resistance to the Soviet maneuver. The question was what the Western powers would do. General Clay, in command in the American zone, was in favor of pushing an armored column through to the capital. But there was an alternative, an alternative hesitantly begun, but developed in a way little short of grandiose. This was the famous airlift. It was begun on the 25th of June, by orders given on the spot, and confirmed by the Department of Defense in Washington. All that was further needed was the approval of the President. When Secretary Lovett saw him on Monday, June 28, Truman made no bones about his position. In fact he interrupted the secretary to state emphatically that there need be no discussion on the main point. "We are going to stay," he said.

The decision of the 28th of June was a vital step in an enterprise that was to last for eleven months. During this period Berlin, a city of two million inhabitants, was supplied by air. There were many sceptics when the airlift was initiated. In November and December, owing to bad weather, air communication was interrupted again and again. In the latter month for fifteen out of thirty days supply was virtually impossible. But in March 200,000 tons of fuel, food, and other materials were flown into the city, and in April the figure rose to 235,000 tons. Planes were landing at intervals of two or three minutes at the two great airdromes of Gatow and Tempelhof. To counter the Russian interference with the supply of electricity, 5,000 tons of machinery were brought in, followed by generating equipment. By the time the Russians confessed defeat and lifted the blockade, it had become clear that, barring interruption by violence, the former capital could be supplied indefinitely, and could even resume to a substantial degree its commercial contacts with the outside world. There could have been no more effective dramatization of the struggle between East and West, and no greater stimulus to the policy of realignment on which the American administration had now embarked.

By their loyalty to the West in the harsh days of the winter of 1948-49 the Berliners had built up a tremendous bank account for the future. The city became a symbol. Those who called themselves realists could point out that Berlin was not worth a war. But in the actual evolution of policy, what was really unthinkable was to abandon the gallant inhabitants of the former German capital to the tender mercies of the Soviet Union. A sentiment stronger than any logical formula bound Berlin to the West and Berlin remains so bound today.

But why did the Kremlin yield? The ground forces of the Western powers were pitifully small, no more than six divisions. The Russians had forces immensely larger. Considering this disparity, why did not the Russians shoot down the cargo planes that were flying into Berlin, and put a stop to the supplying of the city? There is, of course, no definitive answer to this question. It will be a long time before we can explain Russian policy with finality. Not until that Greek Kalends, when the archives of the Russian Foreign Office are opened, will it be possible to analyze with confidence the policies of the Kremlin in 1948 and 1949.

One possible answer is that the Allied powers were exercising their undoubted legal rights in the airlift. But to explain Russian restraint on this basis is to attach extraordinary weight to Russian loyalty to the written word. It will not satisfy the cynical analyst. There must have been more to the matter than that. A better explanation lies in the American possession of the atomic bomb, and in the preparations, not quite complete in the spring of 1949, for explosion of the hydrogen bomb. Despite the fact that we have no record of any threat addressed to the Soviet Union, it seems highly probable that the nuclear power of the United States was a substantial, perhaps a decisive, factor in the situation. Russian policy, as has never been better pointed out than in George Kennan's article in *Foreign Affairs* for July, 1947, is and has been essentially cautious. With time on its side, the Soviet Union has again and again, when faced with the prospect of war, been willing to wait. This may well have been a fundamental factor in 1948-49.

The year 1948 was, of course, a presidential year in the United States. Actual negotiation of the North Atlantic treaty had to wait on the outcome of that election. Yet on the essential points, the two great political parties occupied similar ground. The critique of American policy in Europe was left to Henry Wallace, who ran as a Progressive. His showing in the election was a miserable one. Not only did he poll fewer votes than a Democratic right-wing insurgent group drawn from the South, which nominated Strom Thurmond, but almost half of the million-odd votes he did receive were cast in the one state of New York. With the reelection of Truman to the presidency the way was cleared for the negotiation of the North Atlantic Treaty.

The treaty was signed on April 4, 1949. In a sense, the name was a misnomer. Among the signatories was Portugal, hardly *north* Atlantic, and Italy, not Atlantic at all. But the very wide participation in the treaty is some measure of the apprehension felt in Europe in 1949. Not only France and Britain and the so-called Benelux countries, but Norway, Denmark, and Iceland were among the signatories.

The most difficult question for the American delegation was a constitutional one. The power to declare war was vested in the Congress. Could the Senate commit the nation to war by treaty? The solution was an ingenious phrase which left the question open, but strongly suggested positive action. The United States, and of course the other signatories, bound themselves "to consider an attack upon any one of the parties in the North Atlantic area as an attack against them all" and "to assist the party so attacked by taking forthwith, individually and collectively, such action as each party should deem necessary, *including the use of armed force* to restore and maintain the security of the North Atlantic area." Such language did not absolutely commit the United States, but it was, as we shall see, to be implemented by action which left no doubt of the purposes of the American government.

The North Atlantic Treaty was ratified on July 21, 1949. On the whole what is remarkable is the ease with which this was done. The voice of protest, for the most part, was stilled. Senator Taft, who represented the reluctants, gave away his case, in a sense, when he suggested that instead of the pact, the United States make a declaration similar to the Monroe Doctrine with regard to Europe. General Marshall and Henry L. Stimson expressed themselves strongly in the closing days of debate. The treaty was approved without reservations by the crashing vote of 82 to 13.

What lay behind this remarkable expression of opinion? Shortly and simply, the fear of a Russian incursion into western Europe. Today, one is disposed to believe that the possibility of such an incursion was not great. The Soviet Union had played it very cautiously in the struggle over Berlin. Indeed, to repeat, one may say of Soviet foreign policy in general that it is aggressive, but circumspect, bent on expansion, but carefully reckoning the costs. But in 1949 the Kremlin itself had aroused the nations of the West to common action.

What were the fundamental reasons for the policy of the United States? Or rather how could that policy be most rationally defended? The answer, as it seems to me, lies in the principle of the balance of power. It was most effectively stated to me in a conversation which I had with one of the most distinguished of American diplomats in the winter of 1950. If the Russians were able to command the technological and natural resources of western Europe, he declared, they would dispose of a complex of power so awesome as to threaten American security. To ward off the possibility of such a combination was in the highest interests of the United States.

To translate a general obligation into a concrete organization committed to defense of the European democracies was, naturally, a long and complex labor. In so far as the American government was concerned, events ran for a time in its favor. The concept of an integrated international force was tenaciously advocated by the administration, and especially by its dynamic secretary of state, Dean Acheson. Reservations as to the wisdom of this program tended to diminish with the events of 1950. The invasion of South Korea seemed new evidence of the Communist desire and intention to make trouble for the West. A kind of superheated nationalism, of which one expression was the anti-Communist crusade of Senator McCarthy, made easier the task of the government. Public fear of the ambitions and aspirations of the Soviet Union was, perhaps, never deeper than at this time. The tensions of late 1950 and early 1951 were extreme, scarcely to be understood by those who did not live through those troubled days, and who cannot understand an emotion that they have not experienced. By September of 1950 it was possible for the newly constituted North Atlantic Council, organized to consider implementation of the treaty, to agree upon "the establishment at the earliest possible date, of an integrated force under centralized command, which shall be adequate to deter aggression and to ensure the defense of Western Europe." Not long thereafter, and with little vocal opposition, President Truman announced that General Eisenhower, at that time president of Columbia University, would resign his academic post and become the commander of the forces to be constituted under the resolution cited above.

A second step, equally dramatic, accompanied this appointment. On the 9th of September, 1950, President Truman announced that it was his intention to "make substantial increases in the strength of the United States forces to be stationed in Western Europe in the defense of that area." It was later indicated that these reinforcements would amount to no less than four divisions, thus increasing by 200 per cent the number of American troops then in Europe.

As a result of the President's decision, there took place an important debate in the Senate. Senator Wherry of Nebraska introduced a resolution on January 8, 1951, providing that "no ground forces of the United States should be assigned to duty in the European area . . . pending the adoption of a policy with respect thereto by the Congress." Here, of course, was a direct challenge to the administration, and incidentally but importantly, to the power of the President to dispose of the armed forces on his own constitutional initiative. The discussion which followed covered no especially new ground. But the witnesses for the administration, the secretaries of state and of defense, and the chiefs of staff, brought home to the American people, more emphatically than had been done before, the cardinal importance of the defense of Europe based on solid military and economic considerations. The thesis that we have already stated deserves repetition: that a Western Europe subservient to the Soviet Union would wield power not inferior to that of the United States.

The Wherry resolution was too strong for all but a small number of dissentients on the Republican side, and a modified resolution which came before the Senate specifically approved the appointment of General Eisenhower, the placing of American armed forces under his command, and the sending of four additional divisions overseas. However, an amendment was attached to the resolution stating that "it was the sense of the Senate that no ground troops in addition to such four divisions should be sent to Western Europe . . . without further Congressional approval." The final vote on this resolution was 69 to 21. On the whole, as it seems to me, the action taken should be regarded, despite the amendment, as a powerful expression of public opinion in favor of the policy of the Atlantic pact.

Certainly the events which were to follow in 1952 placed the opponents of the pact in an untenable situation. For when the Republican nominating convention met in the summer of that year, it chose as its candidate for the presidency none other than General Eisenhower himself, whose acceptance of the nomination was largely due to his deep conviction of the wisdom of the American policy, and his fear that the party to which he belonged would be captured by its isolationist wing. By the time Eisenhower took office the American commitment was strong, indeed, supported by the leaders of both parties and by a large part of the American public.

Let us turn back to see what was happening on the other side of the Atlantic. From its very inception, the North Atlantic treaty idea met with some very real obstacles on the part of its European signers. One element was the reluctance of the governments concerned to make substantial economic sacrifices in their own defense. We shall meet with this question again and again as we examine the events of the next decade. It seems reasonable to say here, however, that at no time have the expectations of the United States in 1952 been completely met.

A second question of great importance was the question of what role should be assigned to Germany. From the outset it was clear to the directors of American policy that German units should be included in the proposed international force. Such a decision seemed particularly desirable because it brought Germany into close association with the West. From the outset the military plans of the alliance called for resistance to Russian aggression on the line of the Elbe. How deny to Germany, therefore, a part in its own defense?

On the other hand, there naturally existed in France a deep distrust with regard to German rearmament. A thaw which took place in Franco-German relations in 1951 partially reduced this feeling, but it was still a force to be reckoned with. The answer was found, however (as it seemed), and by the French themselves. It was found in the presentation of the so-called Pleven plan, which called for an international force in which German elements should play a part, but in which they should be under the direction of the Allied command. The exact size of the units was a matter of substantial debate, but by the spring of 1952 the way had been found to an agreement, and there came into existence a treaty creating the European Defense Community. The signatories were France, Germany, the Benelux countries, and Italy. The objective was the establishment of a community "supranational in character, consisting of common institutions, common armed forces, and a common budget." The signatory powers were to contribute armed forces of divisional strength, which would be combined into army corps, whose commands and staffs would be drawn from various nationalities. The direction of this force was put in the hands of an international commissariat assisted by a Council of Ministers with representation for each of the six powers. A Court of Justice and a parliamentary assembly were to be created, the first to decide disputed questions of interpretation of the treaty arrangement, the second to exercise general supervision over the Commissariat.

These understandings, it will be observed, concerned only six of the NATO powers. But the members of the European Defense Community undertook to regard any attack on any one of the NATO countries as an attack against themselves, and conversely the NATO countries agreed to come to the aid of the Defense Community if any of its members were attacked. In addition to this, Great Britain and the United States pledged themselves in a separate declaration to "act in accordance with Article 4 of the North Atlantic Treaty, if any member of the Defense Community were attacked, to station such forces on the continent of Europe, including the Federal Republic of Germany, as they deem necessary and appropriate to the joint defense of the North Atlantic treaty area," "to maintain armed forces within the territory of Berlin as long as their responsibilities require it," and "to treat any attack upon Berlin from any quarter as an attack upon their forces and themselves."

The agreements of 1952 were the high-water mark of internationalism. In their negotiation, we must repeat, the United States gave every encouragement. "I wish to express my profound conviction," declared Secretary Acheson on the signing of the various engagements, "that what we have witnessed today may prove to be one of the most far-reaching events of our life-time . . . the unity of the free peoples of Europe." When the Senate of the United States was called upon to ratify a document committing the United States to the support of EDC, it did so by a vote of 72 to 5. The conception of European unity, which had played so large a part in the Marshall plan, had once more had a strong influence on American policy.

The impulse toward European unification, however, was not to be lasting. For one thing, the Russian situation changed. In March of 1953 Joseph Stalin died. From the government of Premier Malenkov, who succeeded, came intimations of a milder attitude than that of his predecessor. There were those, of course, who believed the competition between the Kremlin and the West to be irreconcilable, and there are those who believe this today. But the fact remains that the harshness of Russian policy had much to do with the trend of American and European policy, and that a shift, whether sincere or not, inevitably raised the question whether there might not be, sooner or later, a possibility of wider understanding. Moreover, in the early fifties there had been deep-seated fear of an actual Russian attack on western Europe. But after 1953 this fear ebbed. It did not ebb so far as to remove from the minds of statesmen the notion of a common defense. No one, or almost no one, went quite so far as that. But it ebbed sufficiently to give freer play to the forces of nationalism in the West.

This was particularly true in France, which, to this day, has been the most sensitively nationalistic of the great European nations. The fact is not difficult to understand. Humiliated in war, the French naturally sought the reestablishment of their self-esteem. With the memory of German arrogance and German victory in war still fresh, the notion of an association with the Reich was still repugnant to many Frenchmen (despite the steps toward an economic entente). And the opposition of France's greatest figure, General de Gaulle (out of power though he was) may well have contributed to French reluctance to ratify the treaty of 1952.

The treaty had been signed, it will be remembered, in May. Months went by and nothing happened. The French Parliament did not act during the rest of the year, or even in 1953. While it hesitated, John Foster Dulles, secretary of state in the Eisenhower administration, rasped French pride by declaring that French failure to act might compel an "agonizing reappraisal" of American policy. We cannot measure the effect of this statement in any mathematical way. It was not, however, a very constructive step. In the summer of 1954 the French Chamber of Deputies rejected EDC.

The United States, after this blow, was disposed to sulk. But there was still powerful sentiment behind the project of European defense. Nothing illustrates the vitality of this sentiment more clearly than the events that followed. Through the initiative of Anthony Eden, British foreign secretary, a way was found to approach the defense problem from another angle, and with success. It will be remembered that in 1948 France, Britain, and the Benelux countries had signed a treaty of alliance known as the Brussels pact. Under Eden's initiative, this was now enlarged by the inclusion of Germany and Italy in a grouping that became known as Western European Union. The members of this group were to contribute forces to NATO: the Germans twelve divisions, the French fourteen. The Germans, as under EDC, undertook not to manufacture atomic weapons, long-range missiles, and certain other types of armament. Moreover, as a check on the possible influence of the Germans on NATO, the power of the NATO high command was much strengthened. No forces were to be deployed without its consent. To further allay French fears, Britain agreed to keep four divisions on the Continent, which could be withdrawn only with the approval of the members of WEU, except in an acute emergency. These commitments were approved in 1955. NATO no only remained intact, but had been strengthened by the addition of German forces. Occupation of Germany was ended and the Federal Republic took its place with the other powers in the defense of western Europe.

At the time these protocols were signed the United States, Great Britain, and France made a public declaration affirming their recognition of the West German government as the only German government authorized to speak for the German people in foreign affairs; they reiterated the principle that an attack on West Berlin would be regarded as an attack on all three powers; and they declared that the final determination of German boundaries must be achieved by peaceful means and by an international agreement.

The arrangements of 1954 were hailed at the time as a great achievement. They were a dramatic supplement to the steps, already outlined, by which West Germany was tied into the economic framework of western Europe. They stand today in their broad lines. It is true (and of this more a little later) that NATO itself has been subjected to considerable strain; yet at no time has the principle of common action against aggression been disavowed, not even by General de Gaulle in his most nationalistic moments. It is important to remember this as we review the history of the period since the signing of the protocols.

The first effects of the arrangements of 1954 seem to have been happy ones. The regime of Malenkov in the Soviet Union seemed at the outset to be looking for means of alleviating the international situation. The aggressive policies of the former dictator had palpably resulted in stiffening the attitude of western Europe. The Russians now had both the atomic and the nuclear bomb. They were in a better position than ever before to realize how calamitous, how catastrophic, would be the consequences of nuclear war. The Russian people were increasingly desirous of some improvement in their economic lot. There was, therefore, a brief period of blandishment, signalized especially by two factors.

The first of these factors was the liberation of Austria from four-power occupation. Numberless proposals looking to this end had been put forward by the Western powers. Suddenly in the spring of 1954 the Austrian chancellor was called to Moscow and told that the time was ripe for the liberation of his country. In June of 1955 the four powers met at Vienna and handed over to the Austrian government full authority, conditional on the pledge of the Vienna regime not to enter into an alliance with any other power, and not to permit the installation of any force on its territory.

The liberation of Austria was followed in July by a four-power conference at Geneva, which met in a hopeful atmosphere. But the German question, understandably enough, proved much more intractable than the Austrian one. The Western powers pressed for the unification of all Germany through free elections, something far beyond the willingness of the Soviet regime to grant; the Russians, on the other hand, seemed to be talking of watering down the defense arrangements of the West, and even of the eventual withdrawal of American forces from Europe.

It was not strange that the Russians were not persuaded to further concessions. It was becoming patent that the construction of a strong NATO force would be a slow business; indeed, before the year 1956 was over the centrifugal tendencies within the Western alliance were obvious.

The occasion was the nationalization of the Suez Canal by the Egyptian dictator, Nasser. To the French and the British, the arbitrary action of the Cairo government called for vigorous action. To the United States, patient negotiation seemed the right course. The details of the story we need not examine. Suffice it to say that in October of 1956 the French and British landed troops in the canal area ostensibly to interpose between the Egyptian forces and the Israeli forces, which had launched an invasion of Egypt (certainly with French and probably with British encouragement). A tremendous storm arose; loud protests came from Moscow, not rendered particularly amiable by its own troubles in Poland and by actual revolt in Hungary; at Washington the French and British action was roundly condemned; and in the debates in the United Nations the Russians and the Americans stood side by side. The rift in the alliance was a wide one, for all the world to see.

The action of the French and the British in 1956 illustrates one of the difficulties in the NATO alliance. The interests of the signatories in many parts of the world are far from identical. For example, the British had recognized the Chinese Communist regime at Peking. The Americans had not. The French had withdrawn from Indochina. The Americans had become the protectors of free South Vietnam, to the chagrin of Paris. But the dissidences did not end here. Even in the European field there were strains and tensions. The Americans had begun with demands for strong measures of national defense in Europe; at one of the first NATO conferences there had been talk of an armed force of ninety-six divisions to withstand a possible assault. Such grandiose schemes met with no positive response. The European members of NATO were more concerned with the health of their economies. They proceeded slowly in building up their armed forces, and were in this regard under constant prodding from the United States.

At the moment at which we stand, NATO is passing through a difficult period. The source of the difficulty lies in General de Gaulle. Of de Gaulle's immense services to France there is no doubt whatsoever. But in an age of increasing internationalism, he is a strong nationalist and a romantic one to boot. It might be unfair to emphasize that there is also a strong element of personal pique in his point of view, but it is evident that the attitude of the British and Americans toward him in the war years was not always a model of tact. Wounded *amour-propre* is sometimes a factor in international relations. However this may be, shortly after he entered office as president, he proposed a three-power understanding with Great Britain and the United States. Rebuffed, he has shown a strong desire to go it alone. Some time ago he withdrew the French fleet from direct NATO control and declined on several occasions to participate in NATO planning and maneuvers. At the same time he has been seeking to develop an independent nuclear force of his own, challenging the American policy aimed at the limitation of nuclear weapons. Now, in 1966, he is demanding that American installations in France be withdrawn, and is planning for France an independent, though a coordinated, role with the other members of the North Atlantic Treaty Organization. His speeches often rasp American susceptibilities. On the one hand, he casts doubt on the willingness of the United States to fulfill its engagements to Europe. With the characteristic French passion for logic at the expense of reality, he fails to see that to express scepticism as to the American purpose is the best possible way to weaken that purpose. Sometimes he goes to the other extreme, and suggests that the United States might rashly invoke nuclear power where the interests of Europe were not involved, and thus pave the way for a general conflagration. His doubts in this regard are reinforced by the independent role that the United States is playing in the Orient, a role that might conceivably involve other powers. His doubts may have been strengthened by the Cuban crisis of 1962, in which the American government, quite rightly as I believe, acted unilaterally and without attempting to integrate its policy with that of its Allies. Here again he sows mistrust.

Yet de Gaulle's actions, when seen in perspective, and viewed with detachment, do not, as matters stand today, seem to threaten the integrity of the alliance. They involve very substantial expense in establishing new command centers, new communications, and new military dispositions. But the notable fact is that no other member of NATO has shown any disposition to break away from the alliance. The difficulties of detail involved in the readjustment will be numerous, but nothing has happened to suggest that they cannot be overcome. De Gaulle himself has more than once reiterated the view that it is the form of the alliance to which he objects, not the alliance itself.

There is, of course, a fundamental problem connected with NATO that demands constant concern. How to reconcile the decisive power that can be exercised by the United States with the necessity for consultation with the representatives of a large number of other nations? One suggestion has been the creation of an international nuclear force under NATO command. But this idea has lost rather than gained ground in the last few years. The situation as it existed in 1966 was well described by McGeorge Bundy in testimony before the Foreign Relations Committee of the Senate. "The Supreme Commander is NATO's top military commander. He is accountable to higher civil authority along two kinds of channels. One is his multiple responsibility to all the Governments of the Alliance, and the other is his direct line of accountability to the President of the United States. The multiple line makes him the agent of the whole Alliance, however imperfect or uncertain its collective judgment may be. The direct line to Washington makes him the agent of the man who is in charge of the main strategic strength of the West."

Is this arrangement workable? In theory, one might doubt. In international affairs, action, to be efficacious, needs frequently to be immediate. One can imagine a situation where there might be divided counsels, and the alliance might be subjected to severe strain. But the best answer to any question is the answer given by experience.

Since 1954 the Russians have frequently been unpleasant in their relations with the West. They mean to be unpleasant. Their object, again and again, is to stir up trouble. In numerous instances they have done so. When, in 1957, American troops

were landed in Lebanon at the request of the existing government, all kinds of fulminations issued from the Kremlin. In the
eruption of the Congo, the Russians did what they could to
counter the forces of order. They had none but kind words for
the revolt in Algeria, which placed so heavy a strain upon the
French economy and upon the national morale. They have in
general sided with the forces of revolution, and anti-Western
nationalism, from Cairo to Hanoi. There has been no concession
to the West, similar to that which was made with the evacua-
tion of Austria in 1955.

But, and this is the cardinal point, only once have they challenged *directly* the Western position in Europe. This was on the
question of Berlin. In November, 1958, Premier Khrushchev
raised the question of the future of the former German capital
in an acute form. The Allied occupation, he declared, was out-
moded. The Soviet Union, he announced, had determined to
hand over to the East German Republic the powers hitherto
exercised by the Soviet government. It would be up to the
Western governments to deal entirely with the latter. If they
chose to interfere with it, for example, in interrupting Western
traffic with West Berlin, they must take account of the possible
consequences.

The discussion that followed was destined to be a long one.
That there were hesitations in forcing the issue was demonstrated by the fact that two weeks later, the Russian leader set
a period of six months for negotiation before carrying out his
announced plan. To this the Western powers responded by a
clear rejection of the Soviet proposition. On the 14th of December the foreign ministers of the United States, Great Britain,
France, and West Germany declared that they would maintain their rights, including the right of free access to West
Berlin, and they also denied Moscow's right to alter the existing
situation unilaterally or to fix a time limit for discussion of the
problem. On the 16th of December the full NATO Council,
representing all the members of the alliance, endorsed the decision of the foreign ministers.

There followed a period of negotiation which it is not necessary to analyze in detail. The Russian government permitted
the six months period to come to an end without taking any
action. In the summer of 1959 Khrushchev came to the United
States, and engaged in an inconclusive conference with President Eisenhower, which resulted only in a plan for a summit
conference to meet the next spring at Geneva. That conference
had hardly begun when it ended in a fiasco. The Soviet government announced that it had brought down an American reconnaissance plane that had been flying over the Soviet Union. In
the face of Khrushchev's demand for an apology, the President
stood firm. In a rage the Russians withdrew, and once again the
resolution of the Berlin question was postponed. But there were
no more important developments until the Kennedy administration came into power. In June of 1961 the newly-elected President of the United States and the Russian leader met in Vienna.
The President made it perfectly clear that the American position with regard to Berlin was not to be shaken. The discussions were heated, and on the part of the Russian even trucu-
lent. The situation was tense. On the Russian side a wall was
erected preventing the flight of East Germans or East Berliners
through Berlin to the West. The administration responded with
caution, but with wisdom. On the 25th of July, within a few
days of the beginnings of the wall, President Kennedy made a
television address. "We cannot and will not permit the Communists," said the President "to drive us out of Berlin, either gradu-
ally or by force." He then declared that he would ask Congress
for an addition of $3.25 billion dollars for the defense budget,
call up certain reserves and National Guard units, provide new
weapons, and further develop the program of civil defense.
This was not all. These declarations were followed by the
despatch of reinforcements to West Berlin. General Clay, who
had been the key figure in the defense of Berlin in 1948-49 was
sent to the former German capital. Clay was to remain there
until April, 1962.

In the face of these indications of American resolution the

Kremlin faltered. It did more than falter. Despite a bit of bluster, it allowed the Berlin question to fade into the background. There has been no crisis over Berlin in the period since 1961.

How shall we sum up the role of NATO during the last seventeen years? On one point it is necessary to be cautious. We cannot assert categorically that a direct physical invasion of the West was prevented by the Atlantic pact. To repeat what has been said, but deserves to be emphasized, what the intentions of the Russians were we have no way of knowing, in the scientific sense, and will have no way of knowing until that remote day when the Russian archives are opened to the world, or until some indiscreet memoirist reveals the actual facts. If we speak in relative terms of a question of this kind, where exactitude is impossible, we may say that the danger of such an invasion was greater under Stalin than under his successors. The involvement of the United States in Korea in 1950 and 1951 placed western Europe in jeopardy. At that time many persons believed in the danger of positive Russian action. But since 1953 there has been little reason to think that an adventurous policy has been favored by the Kremlin.

If we believe that the Kremlin was deterred from aggressive action in the first years of NATO, we should still have to ask whether it was not the existence of American nuclear weapons, rather than the alliance, that exercised a restraining effect. It would be hazardous to dogmatize on this point. But in view of the consistent reluctance of the Western powers to raise their military force levels to what has been asked of them, it seems likely that the real deterrent to action was the nuclear threat, rather than NATO itself.

There are other points on which speculation seems a little less dangerous. The Austrian treaty of 1955 was a clumsy effort on the part of the Kremlin to counteract the tendency toward European solidarity. And the unity of the Western powers with regard to Berlin was certainly an element in preserving the liberties of the Berliners.

We ought, however, in viewing NATO, to go beyond the military questions that are so important a part of it. We ought to regard it, like the Marshall plan, as one of the manifestations of the urge toward European unity. The close association of the European states has, in the last two decades, been brought about in many ways. Those who take the schematic view of the problem, or who see it in terms of a United States of Europe, are not likely to be content with what has been done. But history is very rarely tidy. And in Europe there has been a long history of dissension and of competing nationalisms. Every instrumentality that reduces this dissension and limits the competition and the jealousy is playing a constructive role.

So, too, is every instrumentality that binds the United States to the sister nations of the Old World. Viewed in this light, NATO is one of the many auguries of a more integrated Western society, united by common ideals, by common interests, and by common hopes.

FOUR

American Policy in the Far East

In the minds of some very able men the illusion persists that the development of American foreign policy is, or should be, a rigidly rational process. First, the argument runs, you determine what is the national interest; then you select the policy that best promotes this interest. Keep cool; let no emotional prepossession interfere with your decisions; if you do this, everything will go well. I will not attempt to enquire what the world would be like if man were a coldly intellectual being; it is sufficiently evident that he is not, that he is, as Alexander Hamilton once put it, a reasoning rather than a reasonable animal. I am sure that many values that we all hold precious would go down the drain if cold intelligence really ruled; but the point is not worth prolonged argument. The world is just not like that. There has been ample evidence in the areas of foreign policy that we have already studied to recognize the fact that emotional preconceptions, aspirations, dreams, "principles" powerfully affect the course of policy.

It can, however, be argued that, had the Americans consulted their national interests in coldly intellectual terms, they might never have become deeply involved in the Orient. At the time of the war with Spain (fought for the freedom of Cuba), we woke up with the Philippines in our grasp; the annexation of the islands has been described by one of America's most distinguished diplomatic historians as "the great aberration," and certainly the responsibility imposed upon us by the acquisition of the islands was greater than any positive material interest that we had with regard to them. Men talked of opening up the markets of the East as a result of our presence there; this was then, and is now, as it seems to me, complete and utter nonsense.

Nevertheless, we were there, and we proceeded to develop a strong sentimental interest in China. This interest was based in part upon a wholly exaggerated idea of the commercial possibilities open to us; and it was further sustained by the widespread missionary interest, which, like the commercial dream, seems to have given an exaggerated importance to what Americans could do there. There was a brief period when we sought disentanglement; the Washington and London naval treaties of 1922 and 1930 seemed to signalize our withdrawal from the Orient, and Professor Whitney Griswold, later to be president of Yale University, could argue cogently in 1937 that from the standpoint of both trade and investment our role in Japan was likely to be far greater than in the Middle Kingdom, and that we had no particular reason to cast our weight in favor of the latter.

None the less, we could not divest ourselves of concern for the Chinese. American public opinion was distinctly hostile to Japan in the war that broke out between Japan and China in 1937, and step by step we advanced toward aid to China. In the years that followed 1937 we addressed countless moral homilies to the Japanese, homilies which may well have been satisfying to American opinion, but which were without visible effect in Tokyo. As early as the summer of 1939 we denounced the commercial treaty of 1911 with Nippon. By degrees we put obstacles in the way of Japanese purchase of military supplies in the United States, a policy which had some justification in view of our increasing commitments to Britain in the war with Germany, but which was irritating none the less. In the summer of 1941 we severed all commercial and financial relations, a move which may have been intended to chasten Nippon, but which certainly failed of its effect. In the long negotiations with the Japanese government in 1941, our refusal to recognize the Japanese position in the war with China was a central factor in making understanding impossible. Perhaps all these things were comprehensible in the light of American public opinion. there is little doubt that they were popular. And it may be, too, that in any case, and whatever our policy, the Japanese militarists, more and more inflamed, would have launched an attack on the United States. Yet it has been suggested by one of our most eminent diplomats that if we had not been so concerned to protect Chinese integrity we might conceivably have prevented the catastrophe of Pearl Harbor. This, of course, is hypothetical history, and not to be taken as gospel. But no one can deny that the result of the American policy was to bring us close to the government of General Chiang Kai-shek and to commit us to a profound involvement in the Orient at the end of the war. It is unlikely that any influential American would have advocated a return to complete isolationism, so far as Asia was concerned, after 1945. A diplomacy of complete disinterestedness as to what was going on in that part of the world would have been quite impossible. The projection of American power into the Far East was a fact; it was a fact of immense importance, and from it flowed consequences that we must now examine in this chapter.

In the decade 1945-55 we made far-reaching commitments. We are committed to the defense of Japan. We are committed to the defense of Taiwan. These commitments depend primarily, perhaps almost exclusively, on American naval power. But we are committed on the continent of Asia as well. We are committed to maintaining the independence of South Korea. We have defended the independent existence of South Vietnam. We have a treaty that extends its protection over Thailand. None of these commitments would have been conceivable thirty years ago.

Let us look first at our relations with China. In the war itself General Chiang Kai-shek could hardly be described as a satisfactory ally. He was preoccupied, very understandably, with the Communist power that was rising in northwestern China, and unwilling to commit his troops in large numbers against the Japanese. While some Chinese units fought bravely, victory over the Japanese came largely through American arms. And it left a China in disarray and threatened with the collapse of governmental power. The American government found itself in a dilemma, perhaps we should say a trilemma. It could get out of China. That would, very possibly, be giving up the game to the Communist Chinese, whose power had been steadily growing in the last years of the war. It could seek to impose its will upon Chiang, and to compel the necessary reforms, fiscal, military, and social, that might possibly make China a viable state —in other words, establish a virtual protectorate. That would have been resisted by Chiang, who showed remarkable tenacity, if not in governing, at least in holding on to power. Thirdly, it could have attempted to bring about some kind of understanding between Chiang and the Communists that would have brought peace and strength. This is what it tried to do, and in this effort it failed. In our current perspective, the effort at compromise, which reached its high point with the Marshall mission to China in 1946, was virtually foredoomed. As the example of eastern Europe demonstrated, when the Communists enter a bourgeois government, they enter it to destroy it. There is no genuine desire for understanding; there is an insistent desire for domination.

From every point of view the position was a difficult one. The Chinese armies of Chiang had become demoralized; they were ill-paid; their leaders were often corrupt; they were incapable of sustained offensives. Assistance we did give to Chiang, not as much as we might have, perhaps, but only to see it frittered away. By 1948, when substantial sums were appropriated for aid to the Nationalists, the situation was rapidly deteriorating—as it had been for years. Step by step the Communist armies advanced, and by the end of 1949 they had driven Chiang from the mainland and forced him to take refuge on the island of Formosa.

The collapse of China offered the Republican opposition to the Truman administration a golden opportunity. In 1948 the President had been reelected in a close contest, and the bitterness of defeat had sharpened the partisan spirit. In the frustration widely felt in America at the course of events, it was easy to take a censorious tone, and to ascribe to the incompetence of the administration events that were hardly within its control. The apologia of the Truman regime contained in the White Paper of 1949, though soundly based, did not prevent a powerful movement of criticism. In the winter of 1950 Senator McCarthy of Wisconsin began a series of attacks upon the President and his advisers. The senator from Wisconsin was the nearest thing we have ever had to a national demagogue. Careless of his facts, contemptuous of them, encouraged and supported by many of the foes of the administration, he created a climate of opinion on which we must look back with profound malaise. Playing on the frustrations generated by the situation in the Far East, he harassed the President and his advisers and made difficult a well-balanced policy in the Orient.

At the outset, however, the policy of the government was a cautious one. Despite the agitation of leading Republicans, including ex-President Hoover and Senator Knowland of California, for the support of the Nationalist government, neither the President nor the secretary of state desired such a commitment. On January 5, 1950, President Truman declared that the United States had no intention of "utilizing its armed forces in the present situation" or of providing "military aid or advice" to the Nationalists, who had by then fled to Formosa. On the 12th of January, in an important speech, Secretary Acheson described the defense perimeter of the United States in terms that included the Philippines and the Ryukyus, but excluded Formosa. In all this there was at least an intimation that Chiang would have to shift for himself. It is possible, indeed, that this policy would have been pursued, had it not been for events in another quarter.

Arthur Schlesinger, Jr., has written of the inscrutability of history. An illustration is to be found in the occupation of southern Korea by American forces at the end of the war. The decision was a casual one; it was made at the military level; and it was thought to be temporary, pending the establishment of a free Korea. But events did not fall out that way. In the North, where the Russians held sway, a Communist-oriented government was speedily established; in the south a non-Communist regime (hardly a democratic one) under the aged patriot Syngman Rhee was set up. This government was recognized by the Assembly of the United Nations as a legitimate government.

Despite this fact, the American administration at the outset intended no involvement. Not only were the American forces withdrawn in the summer of 1948, leaving the South Korean regime to face the Communist government in North Korea, but in his speech of January 12th, 1950, Secretary Acheson used language with regard to the area which may have suggested to the North Koreans that the United States would not act vigorously in defense of the South Koreans. Should there be an attack on this area, he declared, "the initial reliance must be on the people attacked to resist it and then upon the commitments of the entire civilized world under the Charter of the United Nations which so far has not proved a weak reed to lean upon by any people who are determined to protect their independence against outside aggression." This language, in fairness to the secretary, should be carefully scanned. It did not suggest complete indifference to the Korean problem. It did not bar the possibility of some kind of positive action. But it was read by the North Koreans in a different context.

Two other episodes in the winter of 1950 may have had a part in shaping the events that were to follow. The first was the rejection by a narrow vote in the House of Representatives of a bill extending economic aid to Korea. Though this vote was later reversed, it might have seemed a signal to the North Koreans to go ahead. The second episode was a speech by Senator Connolly, chairman of the Foreign Relations Committee in the Senate, in which he repeated the Achesonian thesis that the United States was not bound to act unilaterally in the defense of South Korea. How this was received in the northern capital of Pyongyang we do not know, but it is not likely that it passed unnoticed.

However this may be, on the 25th of June, 1950, North Korean forces, acting either on their own or on Russian instigation (probably the former), crossed the frontier and launched a full-scale attack on South Korea. This action was a direct challenge to the authority of the United Nations, for, as we have said, the South Korean government had been recognized as a lawful government by a vote of the Assembly in the fall of 1948.

On the very day of the invasion the United Nations Security Council met to consider the situation. It so happened that the Russian representative on the Council was absent. He had withdrawn as a protest against the failure of the United Nations to recognize the new government of the Chinese People's Republic. The possibility of a Russian veto was therefore excluded.

By a vote of 9 to 0, Yugoslavia abstaining, the Council called for the immediate cessation of hostilities, called upon the North Korean government to withdraw its forces from the soil of South Korea, and called upon the members of the United Nations to "render every assistance to the United Nations in the execution of this resolution and to refrain from giving assistance to the North Korean authorities." This resolution, it will be observed, was cautiously phrased. Had it called for direct military action, it might not have been passed so easily. But the American administration interpreted it as authorizing immediate assistance to the South Korean government. On the 27th President Truman ordered the United States sea and air forces to give the Korean government cover and support. On the 30th he authorized the use of ground units under the command of General

MacArthur to assist the hard-pressed forces of the assailed state. Thus began the Korean war. We shall not here describe the course of the war in detail. At first the defenders were hard pushed. Then General MacArthur, by a brilliant maneuver, one of the most daring in recent military history, got in the rear of the attackers and drove them back in headlong retreat, pushing his advance forces to the Yalu. But in October the Chinese began their intervention. The forces of the United Nations were compelled to retreat. The bitter fighting that followed was ended for the time being by the opening of truce talks in the summer of 1951. These talks, for a time interrupted, finally brought an agreement in the summer of 1953, when the Eisenhower administration had superseded that of Truman. The lines were stabilized; for the most part what was South Korean remained so.

Why did the Chinese consent to an armistice? On the 2nd of February, 1953, President Eisenhower made it clear that the United States would no longer oppose action by the Chinese Nationalists against the mainland (a policy subsequently reversed). Not much later he made it clear that if an agreement was not arrived at, the United States might extend the war to the Chinese mainland, and might have recourse to nuclear weapons. In the meantime, it had become clear to Peiping that it could not count on the Soviet Union to come to its defense. The political situation in Moscow was a confused one. Stalin at the end of February was at death's door, if, indeed (as has sometimes been asserted), he had not already died. At a time of crisis at home, involving the question of the succession, it would have been inconceivable for the Kremlin to involve itself in a struggle with the United States.

Few events in the field of foreign policy have been more interesting to the diplomatic historian than the Korean war, from whatever point of view we regard it.

With regard to the constitutional aspect of the matter, the striking fact is that President Truman acted without a declaration of war in ordering General MacArthur into Korea in June of 1950. The scope of presidential action in initiating hostile action was, in this instance, widened over any previous precedent. That the executive could dispose of the armed forces in such a way as virtually to promote conflict was well established before 1950. President Polk had sent American troops into the disputed territory between the United States and Mexico in 1845, and his action had something to do (though not everything) with the war that followed. President Wilson in ordering the arming of the merchant vessels of the United States in March of 1917 was, of course, inviting a conflict with Germany. President Franklin Roosevelt, in ordering naval action against German submarines in the autumn of 1941, invited an armed response from Hitler. But in each of these cases a declaration of war followed. In the Korean instance, this was not true. The conflict was waged with the full support of the Congress, but not with a formal pronouncement that war existed. Criticism, of course there was, but surprisingly little, considering the momentous nature of the decision. Moreover, the choice before the President was of a somewhat novel character. In the preceding instances we have mentioned the drift of American public opinion was already clear. Per contra, Truman acted boldly and decisively in confronting a foreign policy crisis which no one apprehended, and for which the American people were by no means prepared.

Should he have taken a different course? It is, of course, possible to argue that the President's action was a serious breach of the best constitutional procedure. It is also possible to argue that time was of the essence, and that it would have been folly to wait while the Congress debated the wisdom of the executive's action. It seems fair to say that most students would take the latter view. But we can say more. The action then taken (i.e., military action on a substantial scale without a formal declaration of war) set a precedent that has been followed in several instances—in the Formosa Straits in 1955 and in Lebanon in 1957. Still more striking is the fact that when confronted by the challenge of nuclear weapons in Cuba in 1962 President Kennedy established a quarantine by the navy without the explicit approval of Congress, and risked a direct confrontation with the Soviets. From these examples it would appear that the exigencies of the cold war are altering the nature, or extending the scope, of executive power in international emergencies.

This is not the only question of governmental organization raised by the Korean war. The President's dismissal of General MacArthur has profound implications for our foreign policy, now so largely influenced by military considerations.

The background of this famous controversy needs to be sketched in. Despite the military reverses to which we have attested, MacArthur was, as any general would be, still panting for victory. The administration, on the other hand, feared that deeper involvement would have adverse effects upon the total international situation, that it would disturb our European friends and involve commitments beyond our strength, in view of possible danger in Europe. The chiefs of staff were of the opinion that our resources were not adequate for an all-out war in Asia. Faced with restraint, imposed by Washington, MacArthur not only chafed, but exploded. On the 25th of March, without authority, and while the administration was considering the possibility of negotiations, he declared himself ready to confer with the commander-in-chief of the opposing forces, suggesting that failure to agree (that is, on American terms) might be followed by the expansion of military operations to Red China itself. On the 5th of April, Joseph W. Martin, the Republican leader of the House, read a letter from the general which directly and sharply criticized the policy of the government. On April 10th, incensed at the general's action, President Truman removed him from his command.

That the President's decision took immense courage hardly needs to be argued. The partisan storm that arose in the United States was phenomenal. The general returned to the United

States and addressed the Congress amid wild enthusiasm. Truman's popularity sank to a new low. But this is only the superficial side of the story. The President's action, in broad perspective, was right. The subordination of the military to the civil authority is a fundamental principle of American government. And the principle is more vital today than ever. In a world where the military arm is more important than ever before, it is overwhelmingly imperative that the power of ultimate decision should rest in civil hands. In acting as he did, President Truman performed a servce of transcendent value to the American people.

Let us turn from these constitutional issues to consideration of the impact of the military situation on American foreign policy. The Korean war is the first war in the history of the United States when the United States did not attain complete victory. The armistice signed in the summer of 1953, as we have said, left South Korea virtually intact; indeed, it improved the boundary line on the west, but it left the military situation a stalemate. And it raises, therefore, a question of great import. Have we come to that point in the competition of power where no nation can afford to insist upon the complete subjection of the enemy? Have we reached a point where only limited war is possible? The answer to this question we shall defer for the moment. But we ought to realize why the matter was decided as it was. A land war on the continent of Asia was deemed to be beyond the capacities of the United States. To use nuclear weapons in this instance would have been to shock the public opinion of the rest of the world. To press matters to a conclusion would at the worst, have involved the entry of Russia into the struggle, and in any case would have involved substantial aid from the Soviet Union to the Chinese; and it would have exposed Europe to possible armed action. This second danger may not have been real, but speaking as one who was in Europe in the winter of 1951, I can testify at first hand that it was seriously apprehended.

There is a second aspect of the Korean war, from a military point of view, that deserves attention. The struggle marked the end of the doctrine of collective security in its extended form. By a mere chance, owing to Russian absence, it was possible to get the United Nations Security Council to authorize action under the charter. But such an opportunity is not likely to occur again. Nor, as matters stand today, is there much chance that, in default of action by the Council, the Assembly would support general condemnation of the aggressor. Indeed, even in 1950, there was, in the actual implementation of policy, no wholehearted acceptance of the collective security principle. Small amounts of aid were given by a minority of nations other than the principal combatants; but 90 per cent of the forces engaged were either Korean or American. Nor were most of the members of the United Nations persuaded to common effort when the Chinese Communists entered the war. The broad doctrine of action by all states against an aggressor died in Korea, and it is safe to say that it cannot be revived.

Let us now look at the Korean problem from a somewhat broader point of view. In the first place, it is highly important to note that it illustrates the importance of ideological motives in American diplomacy. The economic interests of the United States in Korea were very small. It has sometimes been suggested that a security interest was involved, that the conquest of South Korea would have been a threat to Japan. The argument does not seem to me convincing. The defense of the island empire against aggression can hardly be said to have depended upon a small extension of Communist power on the mainland. Nor was this point seriously raised by the administration itself. The defense on which the Truman administration rested was that the integrity of the United Nations Charter was involved, and that submission to aggression in Korea would inevitably lead to new challenges to the existing international order. This, of course, cannot be proved. But the hypothesis was not unreasonable. And it underlines the strong bent of American foreign policy to stress broad moral considerations rather than specific and special interests. Those who seek to find an economic motive in every action of American diplomacy are blind to the considerations that actually influence policy.

But what of the practical results of the Korean adventure? What first of all, of its effects upon Korea itself? Here the answer must be that, whatever American interest was served, the interest of South Korea was most decidedly promoted. The South Koreans themselves fought like lions. They had not the slightest desire to be overrun by the North. They have maintained themselves ever since, and have built up a strong military force. There are still American troops in Korea, but the great proportion of the defense would depend today, as it did in 1950-53, upon the valor of the country's own forces.

But how has Korea fared since 1953? For over a decade it was dominated by that tough old patriot, Syngman Rhee, whose government was arbitrary in every sense of the word. When Rhee was overthrown in 1963, a series of generals succeeded, and in 1966 the president and the prime minister were both military men. But after a rather unhappy period, the economic situation seems to be improving. Recently, better relations have been established with Japan. The country's economy is expanding. The day has not yet come when infusions of American aid are not necessary, nor is the balance of trade situation all that it should be. But there is order, and there is peace, the indispensable conditions for both economic and political progress. There is little agitation for a union with the North. As compared with a Communist regime, the government of South Korea appears to be what the South Koreans want.

If we look at the Korean war from a broader point of view, and with special reference to American diplomacy, it is obvious, of course, that after the events of 1950-53, the emotional commitment ran in favor of a policy of involvement in the Far East. In particular, it fixed our relations with the Chinese, both the Chinese on Formosa and the Chinese on the mainland. We have seen that in early 1950 there was some disposition on the part of the administration to keep out of the Chinese problem. But with the opening of the Korean war, the situation changed. In June, 1950, President Truman altered his tone, declaring that the Seventh Fleet would interpose between Formosa and the mainland, to prevent action of one of the parties against the other. In October, as we have seen, came Chinese Communist participation in the war. The bitterness with which this participation was viewed in the United States is not difficult to understand. Not only were great sacrifices extorted from our soldiers, but we had to confess to something less than total victory. And when after long and irritating negotiations an armistice was signed in the summer of 1953, it brought no prospect of reconciliation. The terms of the armistice have been constantly violated; even today the parties confront each other at the little village of Panmunjon, on neutral ground, and engage in interminable wrangles that do little to advance the cause of international understanding. The Chinese Communist regime has taken advantage of the quiet on the Korean front to engage in military adventure elsewhere, and to foment trouble in southeast Asia.

But let us look for a little at the course of events since 1954 as regards our relations with Peking. In December, 1954, the Eisenhower administration signed a treaty of alliance with the government on Taiwan. The treaty was carefully drawn, so that the adherents of Chiang Kai-shek could not draw us into any mad project for reconquest of the mainland. On the other hand, we committed ourselves to the defense of Formosa and the Pescadores. We left cloudy the status of the islands off the coast that were still held by the Nationalists. In 1955 the Communists launched an attack on the most important of these, Quemoy. At this time, President Eisenhower secured from Congress by an overwhelming vote authorization to come to the defense of the Nationalists if he deemed it necessary. Direct conflict was avoided. The crisis petered out, to be renewed briefly in 1958. Since then, all has been quiet, for the most part.

What shall we say of the commitments we have undertaken to Chiang Kai-shek? In terms of strategic interest, there are two possible points of view. Some persons would seriously doubt the indispensability of Formosa to American defense of the Far Pacific, and it will be remembered that Secretary Acheson explicitly excluded the island from the defense perimeter of the United States in his speech of January, 1950. Others would take a contrary view; but one thing is certain. The commitments made have been within the power of the United States to fulfill.

But let us look at the matter from a broader point of view. If we consider the problem in terms of moral rather than material interest, it can fairly be said today that the American commitment to Formosa is a commitment to sustain a regime that has made immense social progress within the last decade. It is hard for some Americans to believe this. The miserable record which Chiang made on the mainland rises up to plague him. Yet the fact is that Formosa today has one of the highest living standards in Asia, that a sweeping program of agrarian reform has been carried through, that its foreign trade is developing rapidly, and that there is no widespread political discontent. We must not, of course, picture an Elysium. But in the broad view, progress has been great. What we know about Communist China does not suggest that Taiwan would have been happier if it had fallen to the legions of Mao Tse-tung.

There remains, of course, in our relations with the Chinese People's Republic the question of recognition, and of admission to the United Nations. The rigidity with which this question is viewed by many people in the United States is matched by the rigidity of the Communist Chinese themselves. It is often argued that to isolate a state of the dimensions of China is a policy of folly, that China is and will be a great force in world affairs, and that not to recognize this is to stick one's head in the sand. The United States, moreover, has been sharply criticized (and in my opinion justly) for refusing until 1961 to permit the question of Chinese participation in the United Nations even to come before the Assembly or the Security Council. But the matter may be stated in other terms. With regard to recognition, it can be argued that little in the way of freer intercourse has been achieved by those nations which, like Great Britain and France, have sent diplomatic representatives to Peking. It can also be said that the United States has long maintained contact with the government of Mao Tse-tung through its ambassador in Poland, who has held many conferences with his Chinese opposite number without effect. Certainly too much should not be expected from the establishment of regular diplomatic intercourse. There was no notable improvement in Russo-American relations when we extended recognition to the Soviet Union in 1933. What followed, indeed, was disillusionment. Finally, were the United States, as matters stand, to offer to exchange ambassadors, it would, in all probability, expose itself to a resounding rebuff. What will be the situation in the future is, of course, another matter.

With regard to admission of the Chinese Communists to the United Nations, the matter is more complicated than is sometimes assumed. At the moment, the Peking government is lavish in its condemnation of the international organization, declares that it does not wish to join, and even incited Indonesia to withdraw. Were its attitude otherwise, there would still be difficulties. In the United States a proposal for two Chinas has often been put forward. At all times this idea has been rebuffed by Peking. To displace the Chinese Nationalists completely would, as matters stand, be the necessary prelude to admission of the Communists, and such a step would be unwelcome to many other governments, not only our own. Admission to the assembly might, in theory, be granted by a two-thirds vote, but there has been no two-thirds majority up to date. As to the Security Council, a most complex procedure would be necessary. It would begin by raising the question as to which of the two Chinese governments was entitled to speak in the name of China. The President of the Council would then have to declare that this was a procedural question, to which the veto did not apply. If he were sustained by a procedural vote (that is, by nine members), then, by a similar vote, the place in the Council could be assigned to mainland China.

It may be that at some time in the future some such maneuver will be attempted. But it is by no means likely at the present time. It would certainly not be wise for the members of the Council to expose themselves to a sharp rebuff, or, to put the matter more clearly, an assemblage of politicians is not likely to wish so to expose itself. At the moment (and the fact should never be forgotten), the isolation of Peiping is a self-imposed isolation. In the United States, there is often a naive view that a show of good will will be met by an equal show of good will on the other side. This is not true in international affairs. Recently the government of the United States offered to admit special classes of Chinese to the United States, and was willing to permit representatives of similar classes to go to China. Its overtures have met with no response.

It is true that we ought not, on this account, to retreat into an attitude of absolute rigidity with regard to Peking. It is plausible to argue that the government of Mao Tse-tung is passing through a very difficult period. A ferocious nationalism reigns in China. The Chinese administration is gravely disorganized. The quarrel with Russia has imported a new atmosphere of bitterness into the foreign relations of the Chinese Communists. It may be that in due course the situation will change. If it does, conversation with the Chinese may prove feasible. Possibly they may be willing to participate in an international conference, as they actually did in 1954. Certainly, to take only one question, the problem of control of nuclear weapons can be fruitfully discussed only if the Peking government consents to its inclusion in any conferences on the subject. One other aspect of our relations with China ought to be mentioned here. In discussions in the Senate in the spring of 1966 concerning our position in Vietnam, there was frequent expression of the fear that we might be drawn into a war with China. The eminent scholars who testified before the Foreign Relations Committee were not, on the whole, disposed to take this danger very seriously. They seemed to feel that the internal situation in China hardly made such a thing likely. It could have been reasonably pointed out that there were serious logistical problems involved in any invasion of Vietnam. There was a railroad line, not a very good one, through Hanoi to the demarcation line in northern Vietnam. But communication south of that point would have been difficult (though by no means impossible for guerilla forces), but not well suited to the movement of large bodies of troops. The situation from this point of view was entirely different from that which existed at the time of the Chinese riposte in Korea, where the Manchurian railways offered an excellent opportunity for a large-scale offensive. Another point (curiously enough, not brought out or at any rate not emphasized in the hearings) was that all-out Chinese effort would inevitably endanger the atomic installations that the Peking government had established in western China, where they had already brought off at least one nuclear explosion. Finally, it was much to be doubted whether the North Vietnamese themselves, unless invaded, would desire Chinese large-scale and direct assistance.

But we are getting ahead of our story. Let us go back to examine the position of the United States in the area that has come to be known as Southeast Asia. Here the commitments of the United States, in one form or another, go back to 1946. These commitments were in substantial degree ideological. The economic interests of the United States were small. But it could be argued that the spread of Communism in this part of the world was a danger to the United States, a danger calling for vigorous action. The point was certainly debatable, but this ought not to blind the historian to the fact that there was substantial support for it, as early as the days of the Truman administration.

The end of the World War had left Southeast Asia in confusion. A substantial part of this area, Vietnam, Laos, and Cambodia, constituting the colony of French Indochina, had been overrun by the Japanese. In 1946 the French sought to reassert control. Their principal difficulties arose in the first of these three areas. There a powerful movement arose under the Communist leader, Ho Chi Minh, who united an appeal to nationalistic sentiment with an appeal for drastic social reform. Fighting against the French began at the end of 1946. The puppet regime set up to oppose the Vietminh in 1949 was powerless to control the situation. With the conquest of mainland China by the Communists, more and more aid went to Ho Chi Minh. The United States was drawn into the struggle, providing the Paris government with economic and military aid. Between 1950 and 1954 this aid amounted to about $500 million annually.

A genuine crisis arose in 1954, with the seige and eventual capitulation of a French garrison at the northern post of Dienbienphu. Discouraged at the movement of the war, the French decided to negotiate. Thus there was convened at Geneva in April a conference representing the east Asian states concerned, and the "big five" of the outer world, the United States, Great Britain, France, Russia, and (note it well) Communist China. The result was a series of agreements for a cease-fire. The independence of Laos and Cambodia was recognized. Vietnam was divided at the seventeenth parallel, with the Communists dominant in the north, and the south under Bao Dai, a French puppet.

This settlement was extremely distasteful to the United States, so much so that John Foster Dulles, the American Secretary of State, absented himself from the closing sessions of the conference. In its discontent the American government sought to erect a barrier against Communist advances in the treaty of Manila. This treaty, setting up the Southeast Asia Treaty Organization, was signed on the 6th of September, 1954. The signatories were the United States, Great Britain, France, Australia, New Zealand, the Philippines, Thailand, and Pakistan. The pact declared that each of the signatories would "recognize an attack on any one of them as endangering its peace and safety, and would meet the common danger in accordance with its constitutional processes." By a separate protocol, South Vietnam, Laos, and Cambodia were placed under the protection of the alliance.

The SEATO treaty, as it came to be called, has proven a much less effective instrument of collective defense than the North Atlantic pact. It was not regarded with warmth by such important Asian nations as India, Ceylon, Burma, and Indonesia. In its actual application to Vietnam, it has not met with any enthusiasm in either France or Great Britain. It does not commit explicitly to the use of armed force on the part of its signatories. It could have been foreseen at the time of its signature that the United States would carry by far the largest part of the burden if a critical situation arose in Southeast Asia. Yet it did afford a legal basis for the action that was to follow.

For a time matters went rather well in Vietnam. The ineffectual government of Bao Dai in South Vietnam was overthrown, and (much to the chagrin of the French), a strong nationalist leader, Ngo Dinh Diem, took over. For a few years it appeared possible that Diem could build a viable regime, especially since he received substantial aid from the United States. But this success did not last. Diem's regime became more and more arbitrary, and the baneful influence of his family greater and greater. The climax came in 1963. Agitation of the Buddhists against his government was met with brutal repression. On the 1st day of November, a cabal of Vietnamese generals revolted; Diem himself was assassinated, and a military junta took power.

Since that time the United States has struggled against profound difficulties in Vietnam. Long before the fall of Diem, the organization known as the Vietcong had begun a guerrilla campaign against the existing regime. There were native elements in this group, but support on an increasing scale came from the government at Hanoi, and from the followers of Ho Chi Minh. By 1963 the number of these forces had risen to at least 40,000, and the guerrillas held no inconsiderable part of the country by day, and more of it by night. By intimidation and murder of public officials, school teachers, and other authorities, they created a situation of the utmost difficulty. And as the military situation became more and more involved, the choice that presented itself to the government at Washington was between abandonment of the struggle, and substantial reinforcement of the American forces in Vietnam. Under President Kennedy the number of American troops there had been, at its height, no more than 16,000. Under President Johnson it had grown, as of the autumn of 1966, to more than 300,000. At the point of writing, the prudent hisorian will abstain from prophecy. All that can be done is to redefine some of the elements of the situation.

The support of American majority opinion seems to be behind the administration in its policies in Vietnam. In the autumn of 1964, following an attack on two American destroyers by North Vietnamese vessels, Congress passed an important resolution. This resolution read as follows: "The United States regards as vital to its essential interests and to world peace the maintenance of peace and international security in South East Asia." It also said, "The United States is therefore prepared as the President determines to take all necessary steps, including the use of armed force to assist any member or protocol state of the Southeast Asia Collective Defense Treaty requesting assistance in defense of freedom." The vote in support of this resolution was overwhelming. Nor was the situation changed by the events of the spring of 1966. In March the Senate Committee on Foreign Relations, under the chairmanship of Senator William J. Fulbright of Arkansas, held prolonged hearings on the situation in Vietnam. There were those like General Gavin, a former ambassador to France, and George Kennan, one of the most distinguished of American diplomatists, who suggested a limited policy, a policy of maintaining American forces in certain enclaves, not precisely defined, and placing upon the Vietnamese army the responsibility for the rest of the country.

But the striking feature of the hearings was that virtually no one suggested an unconditional retreat from South Vietnam. George Kennan suggested a "dignified" withdrawal, but it was difficult to define what a "dignified withdrawal" would be. For the most part, the critics of current American policy were stronger on the negative than on the affirmative side. And when the test came in the form of a vote of additional appropriations for the prosecution of the war, the support of both political parties in both houses of Congress was overwhelming. That this was an unpleasant war was widely conceded; that if the past could be repealed we might have done better not to get involved was widely asserted; but a large body of opinion believed that, since we *had* become involved, there was, at the moment, no way out of the impasse.

There were, of course, those who thought differently. Some people in the United States, and influential people in France, including the President of the Republic, Charles de Gaulle, put forward the idea of neutralization of the area. But the tone of defiance that came from Hanoi did not suggest that any such solution of the problem was feasible.

Before we leave the subject of Vietnam, there are several other points to which we should advert. The conventional rationale for the policy which the United States was pursuing may be described as the domino theory. The supporters of this theory argued that if South Vietnam went down the drain, further calamities would surely follow. "He who holds or has influence in Vietnam," wrote Henry Cabot Lodge, at the time of writing our ambassador at Saigon, "can affect the future of the Philippines and Taiwan to the East, Thailand and Burma with their huge rice surpluses in the west, and Malaysia and Indonesia with their rubber, oil and tin to the south. Japan, Australia and New Zealand would be deeply concerned by the Communization of South Vietnam." Such a position cannot be completely refuted, for it rests upon assumptions that can neither be proven nor disproven. (I do not myself accept it.) It is perfectly possible to take a completely different tack, and to assume that defeat for the anti-Communists in Vietnam would lead to resolute efforts in other lands to take those measures of social and political adjustment that would make the victory of the Communists impossible. We are here in the realm of hypothesis, not that of objective analysis. But, on the other hand, we must frankly recognize that, whether wholly logical or not, the proposition we have just discussed, that is, the domino theory, has been widely held, and that it had in an earlier period the adhesion of President Eisenhower, as it has had the adhesion of President Johnson.

Analogous to this point of view, but perhaps a little more persuasive, is the contention that retreat from Vietnam, and especially an undignified retreat, would shake the national prestige and embolden the Communists to undertake, not necessarily in Southeast Asia, new challenges to the position of the United States. The hesitations of the Bay of Pigs (see p. 132) and the disaster that followed very probably emboldened Khrushchev to the implantation of Russian missiles in Cuba. From this point of view, any position that reveals the weakness of the national will, or casts doubts upon the national resolution, is dangerous and may have unhappy consequences. Here again, we are certainly not in the realm of mathematical certainty. But there is no doubt that the argument has weight with many thoughtful people.

There is, however, another point of view that will to some

people seem more appealing and more persuasive. Having committed ourselves in South Vietnam, can we with good conscience withdraw, and leave the South Vietnamese to the tender mercies of the North, with the resultant social disorganization and Communist tyranny? There are hundreds of thousands of refugees from the North in the South. There is a native population that, so far as one can judge, has been very far from welcoming the forces of Ho Chi Minh or the Vietcong as conquerors. Is no account to be taken of them?

This point of view can be pushed further. Our proclaimed ends go beyond reestablishment of security in the country. They involve not only pacification, but assistance in an economic reconstruction that might bring prosperity to the East Asia region as a whole. The Johnson administration has put forward ambitious plans for building a great dam on the Mekong, and for measures of agricultural development that might be of very profound effect. Some people who would approve of these ends fail to see that economic reconstruction and military victory cannot be separated. It is well enough to speak of the former as if it stood by itself; but the primary condition of economic progress is civil order. You cannot plan the rebuilding of a house if the house is burning down; you have first to put out the conflagration. To overlook this fact is, in my judgment, to take a very romantic view of the problem.

We shall have to close this brief examination of the Vietnamese problem with the conventional reservation of the historian. The plain truth of the matter is that we are not in a position today to pass any definitive judgment on what is happening in this part of the world. It is possible that our venture will involve greater sacrifices than we have hitherto made; that it will prove extremely difficult to provide stable government for South Vietnam and to persuade the external aggressor to desist; that the sacrifices, economic and human, that we shall have to make will become more and more onerous and painful; that those who assert that we have no business on the continent of Asia will insist that they have been proven right by the events of the future. In answer to such prophecies we can only say that at the moment at which we stand, there is no sign that either the administration or the American people have come to any such point of view. We must then, in good conscience, reserve judgment.

We shall end this brief analysis of the situation in the Far East on a more cheerful note. Let us examine the results of the American presence in Japan in the years following the war, and the position of Japan today.

As always, the perspective may change, but it seems fair to say that enormous changes have been brought about in the Japanese social, political, and economic order. Before Pearl Harbor, Japan was ruled by an Emperor who was assumed to be of divine origin. Though parliamentary principles had begun to take root, they had been vitiated by a special relationship in which the ministers of war and of the navy stood to the throne. The military tradition ran deep and strong, as the events of the thirties bore witness. A small number of families controlled most of the wealth, and most of the large peasant population did not own the land it worked. Industrial workers were for the most part unorganized, and after 1928 their organizations had been virtually crushed. Moreover, the secret police exercised a rigid role.

The American occupation that followed the end of the war effected an enormous change in the situation. Under General MacArthur's proconsulship the structure of Japanese political and economic life was profoundly altered. The Emperor became a ceremonial head of state, no longer a god, and the shrines for his worship were closed. A democratic constitution was drawn up, on the basis of parliamentary responsibility. A bill of rights was framed. The courts were reorganized. These political changes were followed by economic changes, of which the most important was the agrarian reform law of December,

1945. This law enabled Japanese farm workers to become the owners of their own land. Absentee landowners were compelled to sell their land to the government, which parceled it out to the peasants, who then paid for the property. Where land was not actually taken away, rents were drastically reduced. The creation of an independent class of small proprietors, it was prophesied, would consolidate and fortify the democratic principle in Japan. No nontotalitarian nation has ever carried out a more sweeping measure of orderly change, and after twenty years the change has stood.

There were other significant reforms in the years of the occupation. The great industrial combinations were to some degree broken up; a countervailing power was created by the recognition of collective bargaining and the creation of labor unions. The educational system was reorganized and strengthened.

The occupation, in the sense of power imposed by the United States, ended with the Japanese peace treaty in 1951. This treaty, signed on the 8th of September, 1951, was an extremely wise one. The United States demanded no reparations; on the contrary, in the period immediately following, the United States granted economic aid to Japan. In a collateral arrangement, the Japanese agreed to the maintenance of American armed forces in Japan with a view to protection of their territory. Prime Minister Yoshida declared that his country "gladly accepted" this fair and generous treaty which, he stated, "was marked by a magnanimity unparalleled in history."

Since 1951 Japan has staged one of the great economic comebacks of the postwar period. The war in Korea acted as a stimulus to its economic recovery. With amazing ingenuity, the Japanese turned to the task of developing their international trade on a wider basis than ever before. The problem of overpopulation (a serious one) was met by drastic methods of birth control. Among the nations of the Far East, Japan today seems to stand pre-eminent in the strength of its institutions and in the growth of its economy. Rebirth of the old militarism is hardly to be apprehended.

On one question friction could conceivably arise between the United States and Japan. The United States now exercises control of the island of Okinawa, one of the principal bases of the United States in the Pacific. There was incorporated in the peace treaty a provision by which the Japanese government agreed to concur in any proposal to the United Nations to place the area under trusteeship. No action, however, has been taken in this regard. The United States has remained in exclusive control. On the other hand, agencies of local government have been established. A chief executive is appointed by the American high commissioner, there is an elective legislature and an independent judiciary. There has been no deep-seated political discontent, and no real friction with Tokyo. But there are possibilities of an unpleasant kind; and a revival of Japanese nationalism might create, with regard to Okinawa, a disagreeable situation. On the other hand, Japan's interests are so closely tied to the interests of the United States in the Far Pacific that it is possible to take an optimistic view of this problem.

We stated at the outset of this chapter that the interest of the United States in the Far East rests to a substantial degree on emotional grounds. The events of the last thirty years have only strengthened the feeling to which we have referred. The power position of the United States in the Pacific is a very strong one. In terms of naval force we have, of course, no rival, and are not likely to have one. With regard to Vietnam, as we have already said, suspended judgment seems necessary. But if the American position is ever shaken it will be by events which we cannot as yet foresee, involving drastic political changes, in Taiwan, for example, with the death of Chiang Kai-shek or in Korea as a result of internal convulsion. It is sometimes said that the United States of 1966 has taken on larger responsibilities than it can afford to carry. There is nothing in the situation today to prove beyond possibility of rebuttal that this is true.

And whether true or not, it is highly unlikely that the position which we occupy today would be willingly abandoned. As a postscript to this observation, we ought to add that we have treaty obligations today that tie us to Australia and New Zealand. These obligations are another reason why we shall not, in all probability, reduce our role in the Far Pacific.

FIVE

The United States and Latin America

The relations of the United States with Latin America were on the whole remarkably happy during the years of the Second World War. Most of the states broke relations with the Axis early in the struggle; only Argentina hesitated until almost the end. Many of them, especially the Caribbean states, declared war, and the prosperity that these states enjoyed during the world struggle added to the euphoria of the period. This attitude, foreover, carried over after the conflict had ended. Pursuant to reigning theory, the United States entered into a collective security arrangement with the Latin American states by the treaty of Rio, signed in September 1947. The treaty followed the pattern already set by the Charter of the United Nations. It called for common action in meeting aggression against any of the signatories, the character of the action taken to be determined by the organ of consultation, and a two-thirds vote to be binding on all. It was hailed at the time as a great achievement, and it was ratified by the Senate of the United States by an overwhelming vote.

In the perspective that we have today, there is little reason to take the Rio treaty very seriously as a defense against an assault. A direct physical attack on any one of the Latin American states was among the least likely dangers that could be conjured up; and even if such an attack occurred, it was obvious that the burden of repelling it would rest almost wholly on the United States, and of course, the attacked state. The military and naval establishments of most of the states were small; in the nature of the case, they could play but a minor role.

What was much more to be feared than invasion was subversion, and here both ideological and economic interests were involved. For American investments in Latin America in 1945 were larger than in any other great geographical area (save Canada); and though they have since been outdistanced by our investment in Europe, they are still of far greater importance than those on the Asiatic continent or in Africa. What was true of investments was true also of trade. Even including Japan and the Philippines, as late as 1954 the figure for Latin America was 70 per cent greater than that for Asia. Devotees of the economic interpretation of history have found some confirmation for their viewpoint in our relations with our southern neighbors.

There was also an ideological connection with Latin America. It is true that few Latin American states have not the record of political stability and orderly democratic progress that distinguishes the United States; but it is also true that democratic ideals have played a part in their evolution, and that the appeal to democratic principles has figured importantly in our foreign relations with these lands. The existence of the Pan-American Union since 1889, and of its successor, the Organization of American States, created in 1948, is an indication of a sense of solidarity which is significant in inter-American relations.

At the same time we must take account of the forces that divide as well as the forces that unite, and that make the threat of subversion something to reckon with. In the first place, the physical power of this country produces an inevitable malaise. It is true that on the whole, during the last thirty years, we have used that power with restraint, but the Latin Americans remember our inerventions in the period stretching from 1912 to 1934, and have a nervous dread of new attempts at domination.

Moreover, there are rifts in the lute on the economic side. American markets are valuable and for some of the states indispensable; but the terms of trade are a frequent source of irritation. The principal exports of the Latin American states are staples, the prices of which have historically been subject to frequent and often violent oscillations. We cannot, of course, be blamed for this with any justice; but we *are* blamed when rising prices in the United States increase the cost of the commodities that Latin America buys in this country, while declines in the prices of the raw materials they sell yield them a poor return on their exports.

In addition, there is a legend, not necessarily confined to Latin America, that American capitalism is a menace to the development of other lands. I say "legend," because the exportation of American capital to foreign countries has, on balance, done much more good than harm. (The Canadians will testify to that.) Yet it is not strange that some of the southern republics, especially those that are poor, view with some apprehension the power of American business men as a justification for their attitude. It might reasonably be said today that the thing for Latin America to do is to welcome American capital, and then regulate it and tax it to the degree that the interests of the capital-receiving state dictate; but rationality does not always rule, and it has not been difficult for the propaganda of the Left to make an impression on the Latin American mind.

Hostility to American capital, where it exists, is buttressed by the social situation in many, perhaps most, of the Latin American states. The immense gulf between rich and poor that exists in most of them, the selfishness of large elements of the ruling classes, taken collectively (of course there are many instances of individual concern), the misery of city slums and of the peasantry—all offer a fertile field to unrest, which finds in the United States an object of distrust, aversion, or even hatred. That such a sentiment is characteristic of the majority one would not contend; but it exists in a minority and it can be manipulated by those who seek drastic social change. Thus one of the themes of this chapter must be the question of what has been done, and is being done, to assist the nations of the south in the development of their economies and of their social order. Let us look first, however, at the question of Communism. There have been, as we all know, two occasions on which Communism has directly challenged the United States, one in Guatemala and one in Cuba. First as to Guatemala. Historically, Guatemala has been governed by caudillos, or personal leaders, invariably military men. But in 1944 the then caudillo, Jorge Ubico (by no means as bad as he has been painted by his enemies), was overthrown by a revolution that brought to power a government under President Arévalo that leaned to the Left. Arévalo was no Communist, but penetration of the government by Communists certainly began in his regime, and though this penetration was far removed from complete control, it offered a prelude to what followed. In 1950 Arévalo was succeeded by Jacopo Arbenz, and the movement toward the Left was accelerated. More and more Communists entered the government, and in 1952 there was passed an agrarian reform law that led, among other things, to expropriations of American property on a substantial scale, especially the property of the United Fruit Company, which had extensive interests in the country. The classical tactic of the Communists has been first to appeal to the peasantry, and then to enslave them. In the case we are considering there was much free land open to settlement; there was little unrest among the agrarian elements themselves; the issue was a manufactured issue. And the administration of the so-called reform was accompanied by violence and corruption on a substantial scale.

Was it Guatemalan action against United Fruit that prompted the hostility of the American government to what had occurred? It would be too much to expect that Washington, in a case of this kind, would observe an Olympian detachment;

but to assume that a specific economic interest was all that was involved would be an error. Ideological opposition to Communism was never stronger than in the early fifties, and no public official has been more sensitive to the ideological challenge than was the secretary of state of the epoch, John Foster Dulles.

At any rate, it was some time before the administration revealed to the American and world public its distaste for the Guatemalan regime. It did so at the Inter-American Conference of Caracas, which convened in March of 1954. There Mr. Dulles introduced a resolution, a relatively mild one, declaring that the "domination or control of the political institutions of any American state by the international Communist movement, exending to this hemisphere the political system of an extra-continental power, would constitute a threat to the sovereignty and political independence of the American states, endangering the peace of America, and would call for a meeting of consultation to consider the adoption of appropriate action in accordance with existing treaties." It cannot be said that this resolution was a very sweeping commitment. The fact of the matter is, as we have said, that the Latin American states have frequently feared American intervention almost as much as they fear Communism, and have been slow to recognize the Communist danger when it appears. At Caracas, indeed, while they voted with the United States, their hearts were with Guillermo Toriello, the Guatemalan foreign minister, when in an eloquent speech he excoriated American imperialism. The Uruguayan delegate was not far wrong when he said to a reporter, "We contributed our approval without the feeling that we were contributing to a constructive measure." Nor was the position of the United States improved when it abstained from voting on an anticolonial resolution, or when Panama introduced a resolution condemning racial discrimination.

But, as has happened so many times, the forces of the extreme Left overreached themselves. It may not have mattered much that in May the hand of the Guatemalan government was evident in the support given to a strike of banana workers in Honduras, but it was something else when the State Department announced on the 17th of that month that a shipload of arms from the Soviets was on the way to Guatemala, and that the shipment, to quote the Costa Rican ambassador at Washington, was "clearly excessive" so far as Guatemala's domestic requirements were concerned. The American government was now thoroughly alarmed. It sent arms to both Honduras and Nicaragua and it demanded a meeting of the Organization of American States. The Guatemalan government riposted by bringing the whole question before the Security Council of the United Nations; but that body, by a vote of 10 to 1 (the Russians using their veto), made clear the view of its members that the proper forum for consideration of the matter was the OAS. By this time the Latin American states had become aroused to the danger. On the 23rd of June, the Inter-American Peace Committee approved a proposal put forward by Nicaragua calling for a fact-finding commission to investigate the Guatemalan charge of aggression. The Guatemalan government, in a thoroughly imprudent act, then launched a direct appeal to the Soviet Union, ignoring the position taken by both the Security Council and the Organization of American States. But a few days later the Arbenz government was overthrown by a revolution led by Colonel Castillo Armas, and launched from the territory of Honduras. It was only a matter of days before the anti-Communist leader entered the capital in triumph.

The intriguing question with regard to the overthrow of the Arbenz regime and the events that followed is what was the rôle of the United States. To cynical Europeans the ousting of Arbenz was due entirely to the machinations of the American government. This is certainly not true. Fundamentally, the ousting of the proto-Communist regime came from within. It was the refusal of the army to march against the insurgents that cooked Arbenz's goose. Discontent with his regime had existed for some time before the events just described; on at least three occasions the military leaders had called on the President to express their disquietude with his policies, and to interrogate him as to his future plans; on all of these occasions they received no satisfaction. In turning against him, they determined the fate of the government. In doing so, they were no doubt influenced by a general dislike of Communism; but they must, one would think, have been still more disturbed when the President raised the question of arming the workers and the peasantry in his defense.

To these fundamental facts one other must be added. The counterrevolution of June, 1954, was accompanied by no important disturbances among the supposed beneficiaries of the revolution, or in any substantial part of the population. Without being categorical on the subject, this seems to suggest that the Arbenz government was not so much responding to deep-seated popular discontent, as that it had been captured by a revolutionary group that was serving objects of its own. The overthrow of the regime, it must be repeated, was due, not to the strength of the opposition, but to its own inherent weakness.

To say this is not to say that the United States had no part in the events we have just narrated. It is well known that the Central Intelligence Agency was active in promoting opposition to the Communists. Mr. John E. Peurifoy, the American ambassador to Guatemala City, was a vigorous and able man, and it is not to be supposed that he was idle. On the day of the overthrow of President Arbenz, he had conferred with the army chief of staff, Colonel Diaz, endorsed the movement to get rid of the President, and offered strong advice as to the desirability of excluding the Communists from any government that might be formed. He used his very considerable influence to promote an understanding between Armas and Colonel Monzón, who, after a brief interval, succeeded to authority in Guatemala City, and in persuading Monzón to relinquish the presidency in favor of his rival.

Did the American government supply arms to the Armas

forces? Naturally this charge has been made. In a literal sense it does not appear true. But it seems probable that the United States supplied the Honduran government with two bombing planes, and that these—or planes substituted for them—did attack Guatemala City, spreading terror there. But behind the allegation of American aid, there lies a deeper question; just how seriously are we to take an attempt to install a Communist government in the New World? Are we, in all circumstances to stand by and let matters take their course? Or may we not only in our own interest, but in the interest of the Latin American states themselves, take such action as seems feasible to prevent the installation of a government that will most certainly bring with it much suffering and much economic disorganization, and that will have an incalculable moral effect on other republics? These are questions that every individual must answer for himself, but they are not to be brushed aside lightly. I shall have more to say on this matter later.

We must now turn to the question of Cuba. And here the story begins with some analysis of the political and social situation in that republic, and of the revolution that brought Fidel Castro into power at the turn of 1958-59. That revolution has been frequently misrepresented and misunderstood, interpreted as a social revolt against a narrow and selfish oligarchy in which American interests were well represented. That the social situation in Cuba in 1958 was all that the heart could desire no man would maintain. But the fact is that, on a relative basis, Cuba was one of the most prosperous of the Latin American states, with a per capita national income rating below only Chile, Uruguay, Argentina, and Venezuela. There existed in the island a substantial middle class, and a higher level of education than in any other state in the Caribbean. The labor unions were strong, and their interests were given substantial consideration by the Batista regime. The discontent that finally resulted in the overthrow of the existing government stemmed from political, rather than social, factors, and was connected with the increasing and brutal repression practiced by the President. It was accompanied, naturally enough, by proposals for social reform, but reforms carried on within the democratic framework. It was a middle-class movement to a considerable extent. And it certainly was *not* an agrarian revolt.

Of Castro in his prerevolutionary phase, it is difficult to speak with assurance. Like most politicians in search of office, he spoke in general terms, and practiced a good deal of equivocation. He certainly led many people to believe that his advent to power would be followed by new and honest elections. He preached reform, but within the context of the constitution of 1940. In his pursuit of office, he deceived many people who loathed the Batista tyranny, and who genuinely believed in the desirability of change.

For the matter of that, he had his friends in the United States. The influential journalist Herbert L. Matthews, writing for the *New York Times*, sympathized strongly with his announced objectives. In the State Department itself there was increasing discontent with the Batista government, and a hope that a better regime might come into power. Indeed, it may be contended that the action of the American government had a substantial influence in the final collapse of the Batista regime. In the course of 1958, Washington cut short military aid to Cuba. We cannot measure the significance of this event with precision, but it seems not at all unlikely that it shook the prestige of the Batista forces, and contributed vitally to the collapse of military morale. Castro's small army did not win victories in the field; it entered a vacuum left by the dissolution of the regular military machine.

When Castro took power in the winter of 1959, the disposition of the United States was not unfriendly. It is not even certain that American aid might not have been extended to the new regime had Castro been of a mind to accept it. Instead, from the beginning, his government took another tack, displacing and driving into exile many moderate men, imprisoning many others, declining to set a date for the promised elections, extending more and more control over the press, permitting and encouraging the capture of the Cuban labor movement by the Communist elements, accusing the American government of bad faith, even rigging a flight of so-called American planes over Cuba to arouse distrust of the government in Washington, and declaring, quite gratuitously, that Cuba might have to defend itself against the United States with weapons in hand.

The year 1960 saw a further deterioration in Cuban-American relations. Castro was becoming more and more the troublemaker of the Caribbean, organizing expeditions—entirely unsuccessful, fortunately—against other states, welcoming the Russian vice-premier, Mikoyan, to Havana, and establishing diplomatic relations with the Soviet Union and its satellites. In June the Cuban government demanded that American oil refineries refine Soviet oil and when this demand was refused, the refineries were seized. In July a nationalization law was passed, authorizing the expropriation of American properties in general. It is not strange that the Eisenhower administration was moved by increasing hostility to Havana, and that Congress authorized the President to cut the Cuban quota of sugar imports into the United States. On the 8th of July the measure passed both houses and was signed by President Eisenhower. Imports of Cuban sugar were virtually stopped for the rest of the year. Such a step was virtually decisive. The actual breach came, however, in January, 1961. The occasion for it was an insulting demand on the part of Castro that the American embassy at Havana be reduced from 300 to 11 men within forty-eight hours, and that the rest of the American personnel leave the island.

Before the Eisenhower administration left office, it had committed itself to a project that was further to exacerbate the situation. As early as March, 1960, it had begun, through the Central Intelligence Agency, to encourage the Cuban refugees to undertake the invasion of their country. A Cuban training center was set up in Guatemala and a force made ready to land on the coast and attempt the overthrow of Castro. There was never any thought of direct American intervention; the Cuban refugees, it was optimistically assumed, once put ashore, would have little difficulty in rallying the Cuban people to their support.

There have been few projects in the history of the United States that were less successful. The Kennedy administration, when it took office, could hardly abandon the project. On the other hand, the President himself had little heart for it. The intelligence on which the plan was based was pitifully inadequate and inexact. The actual execution of the scheme was a chapter of mistakes. The impending invasion of the refugees was clearly indicated by the activities of the press; an air raid that preceded the actual landing not only gave ample warning to Castro, but was unsuccessful in working adequate damage on his air force; a second air strike on the day of the landing was abandoned for fear of international involvement; no assistance was given to the Cubans by the American vessels that had convoyed the invasion forces to the landing place; and the pitifully small force of the invaders was overwhelmed and destroyed by the forces of the Cuban dictator. An astute student of the landing has described it as one of those rare events in history—a perfect failure.

It seems highly likely that the disaster of the Bay of Pigs— as it came to be called—had important repercussions in Moscow. It may well have convinced Khrushchev, the Russian leader, that the United States would offer no effective opposition to the project that he was now to undertake, the installation in Cuba of missile weapons capable of reaching a substantial area of the United States and a substantial area of Latin America. In adverting to this matter, we come to one of the most remarkable and significant episodes in the recent diplomatic history of the United States, the great confrontation of October 22, 1962.

The story of this confrontation has been told in detail by two members of the Kennedy administration, by Arthur M. Schlesinger, Jr., in his *Thousand Days*, a brilliant historical account, and by Theodore Sorensen, whose close relationship to the President gives his narrative a fundamental importance. I shall, therefore, narrate the actual course of events with considerable brevity, and then turn in somewhat more detail to the implications of this far-reaching event.

The Russian government operated clandestinely with regard to its plan; it did not hesitate to deny that it had any offensive purpose in view; as late as October 13, 1962, Mr. Gromyko, in a personal conference with President Kennedy, reiterated the pacific assurances given by the Kremlin.

None the less, by September, rumors began to become more and more common that something was happening in Cuba. As early as September 7 the President asked Congress for authority to call up reservists to the number of 250,000. On the 13th he stated explicitly that if the security of the United States were threatened, everything necessary would be done to protect the people of the United States and their allies. On the 26th, acting in support of the President, Congress passed without debate a joint resolution declaring that the United States was determined "to prevent by whatever means necessary, including the use of arms, the Marxist-Leninist regime in Cuba from extending by force or the threat of force its aggressive or subversive activities to any part of this hemisphere; to prevent in Cuba the creation or use of an externally supported capability endangering the security of the United States; and to work with the Organization of American States and the freedom-loving Cubans to support the aspirations of the Cuban people for self-determination." On the 2nd of October the Organization of American States, acting on the initiative of the United States, adopted a similar declaration.

In the face of a rising danger, the administration waited until it had all the facts in hand, as revealed by aerial reconnaisance of the island, which clearly showed the existence of missile sites and the presence of intermediate nuclear weapons. Complete secrecy as to the intentions of the Ameriican government was maintained. The President took the nation by surprise when he addressed it on the evening of October 22. His words were as somber as they were clear and resolute. Placing the facts before the American people, he declared: "This secret, sudden clandestine decision to station strategic weapons for the first time outside Soviet soil is a deliberately provocative and unjustified change in the status quo which cannot be accepted by this country if our courage and our commitments are ever to be trusted by either friend or foe." He then proclaimed a strict quarantine of all offensive military equipment under shipment to Cuba, and directed the navy to enforce this quarantine. "Should these offensive military preparations [on the part of the Russians] continue," he went on, "further action will be justified. I have directed the armed forces to be prepared for all eventualities." In another forceful sentence he declared: "It shall be the policy of this nation to regard any nuclear missile launched from Cuba against any nation in the Western hemisphere as an attack by the Soviet Union on the United States requiring a full retaliatory response on the Soviet Union." Finally, he demanded the removal of the Russian missiles from Cuba under international inspection, and, for full measure, the removal, also, of Russian bombers on the island.

Five hectic days followed. On October 23 the Organization of American States endorsed the position of the United States. On the same day, in a powerful speech, Adlai Stevenson, speaking in the Security Council of the United Nations, indicted the Russian government. Returning to the attack in a second meeting on the 25th, he directly challenged the Russian member of the Council to affirm or deny the presence of missiles in Cuba. "You can answer 'yes or no,' " he declared. "Don't wait for the translation. You have denied that they exist—and I want to know whether I have understood you correctly. I am prepared to wait for my answer until Hell freezes over if that is your decision. I am also prepared to present the evidence in this room." The Russian shuffled and evaded.

Some days of suspense followed. But on October 28, Khrushchev yielded. He agreed to remove the weapons of which the United States complained, and also to remove the substantial number of Russian bombers that had been placed in Cuba. Removal of the missiles took place under the inspection of the American navy. The international inspection that the President had asked for did not come about. Castro, understandably irked by the abrupt retreat of the Kremlin, was adamant against any such project. But not much should be made of this point. It has been entirely possible to keep Cuba under aerial reconnaissance, and thus to make sure that no repetition of the policy of 1962 takes place. There have been occasional blusterings from Havana, but we may be very sure indeed that they are blusterings, and nothing more.

The confrontation of 1962 suggests all sorts of interesting questions. The first of these is as to the necessity of the action taken. It has been suggested that, in view of the immense nuclear armory of the United States, the presence of Russian missiles in Cuba brought about no fundamental alteration in the existing situation. The risk of an attack on the United States remained the same as before; it would still have been possible to wreak colossal destruction on the Soviet Union. This point of view ought to be rejected on both general and specific grounds. It contains a grain of truth, but *any* change in the balance of power would inevitably have some effect on the capacities of the United States to defend itself. More important, however, is the moral argument. The youthful generation often thinks little of the lesson so strongly etched in experience in the 1930's, the lesson that one act of violence leads to another, that weakness brings new challenges, and that retreat in the face of danger produces new demands. Some of us remember that France and Britain, having yielded when, had they stood firm, German aggression might very well have been checked, were driven to action when the cards were stacked against them, and undertook the fateful engagements with regard to the defense of eastern Europe that brought them into war under the most inauspicious circumstances. Only those who believe that there is no limit to what one should yield before the threat of another power can reasonably criticize the stand taken by the Kennedy administration.

Yet there were those who were looking for compromise in October, 1962. Walter Lippmann, one of the most respected and most read of American columnists, suggested in the midst of the crisis that the United States offer to evacuate its bomber bases in Turkey in exchange for the necessary concessions on the part of the Kremlin. Whether on this account or not, in the hectic days preceding the final solution of the problem, contradictory notes were received from Khrushchev, one hinting at surrender, one raising the question of the Turkish bases. The administration was confronted by a dilemma and one, that, if less ingenuity had been displayed, might have been highly embarrassing. With remarkable *sang-froid*, President Kennedy and his advisers decided to take for granted the Russian note that hinted at withdrawal, and to leave unanswered the one that suggested a bargain.

Here again, it is possible to pose a question whether it would have done any harm to have accepted the second proposal. It was probably true that the Turkish bases had ceased to have a very great importance in the American plans for the defense of Europe. But to have permitted to the Russian leader this strategic retreat would have been to diminish the immense moral force of the American action. And since it did not prove to be necessary, we can with a clear mind accept the position taken by the administration.

But this is only the beginning of the necessary commentary on the confrontation itself. We must note as a fact of great importance that the decision rested wholly and inescapably on the broad shoulders of the President of the United States. The responsibility was indeed awesome, but it was accepted. Just as Truman in 1950 acted with regard to Korea without waiting to consult the Congress, so Kennedy acted in 1962. He had, it is true, the Congressional resolution of late September as a possible encouragement to vigorous action, but the fact remains that he exercised wide presidential power without calling for the approval of the legislature. His action was taken, moreover, in deepest secrecy. During the days preceding his presidential address, he gave no hint of his purpose. On the week-end before the broadcast, he campaigned in the Middle West, and his return to Washington was declared to be due to the fact that he had a cold. On the crucial day, as Arthur Schlesinger has recorded, he "had an appointment with Prime Minister Obote of Uganda as if he had nothing else on his mind and all the time in the world. Angier Biddle Duke of the State Department remarked to Obote on their way back to Blair House that a crisis of some sort was imminent; the Ugandan was incredulous, and when he heard Kennedy's speech that evening was forever impressed."

A word should be said about the cooperation of the American press. On two occasions, the *New York Times* killed a story that might have embarassed the administation. On the second of the instances, the President called the publisher of the *Times* personally to say that publication might lead to premature action on the part of the Kremlin. It was not that Kennedy's plans were totally unknown, but the surprise effect of the President's announcement was undoubtedly enhanced by the prudence of the editorial room.

Pondering on this, one may well come to the conclusion that the secrecy surrounding the President's action was a substantial element in its success. Had the President appealed to Congress for direct approval, it is by no means impossible that dissenting voices would have been raised. And it is an observable fact that the totalitarian states, completely unfamiliar as they are with the character of American democracy, and with the leeway given to dissent even in the most critical situations, have time and again grievously miscalculated the strength of American will and the basic unity of the American people.

Another interesting point about the decision of October 22, 1962, is that it represented an innovation in international procedure. What was done, it should be made clear, was not to blockade Cuba. Russian vessels, carrying all kinds of supplies, were not debarred from their mission. What was done, we must repeat, was merely to declare a quarantine, by which vessels carrying nuclear missiles were to be stopped and turned back. In the journal, *Foreign Affairs,* a few months after the crisis, an ingenious legal argument was put forward to justify the American action; but like the elaborate defense of the famous bases-destroyer deal of 1940 (by which the United States transferred fifty over-age destroyers to the British), the reasoning seems just a bit labored. This is not to say that the action was not wise; it is merely to hint at the fact that it transcended purely legal considerations.

More important than any of the matters we have mentioned was the wisdom displayed in making the decision. After all, in those hectic October days, there were other courses of action possible. The idea of a direct air attack on the Russian sites was seriously considered. More than one of the wisest and most experienced of President Kennedy's advisers at one time or another favored such a step. But not only was this course of action rejected, but everything possible was done to allow the Russians room for maneuver. The Russian vessels on their way to Cuba with the missiles were allowed to proceed toward the island in order to allow the Kremlin time for reflection; the interception took place, not at the earliest moment, but at a later one. It is important to emphasize this technique. For in such a moment as that of October, 1962, it would have been easy by brusque action to intensify the question of national prestige that was involved. It is fair to say that the restraint and wisdom displayed by the administration should serve as a model for future Presidents, if they have the misfortune to face a crisis of similar magnitude.

With regard to the Great Confrontation, it will be best to analyze its effect on our relations with the Soviet Union in the closing chapter. But it may be stated here with a good deal of confidence that the Russian gamble immensely lowered Russian prestige in Latin America, and made more evident than before the selfishness and the duplicity of the Soviet Union, and the perils that a complacent attitude toward the Kremlin might bring in their train. The Communist movement in the Western hemisphere had been for some time in decline; the decline was further promoted by the maneuver of the Russian leader.

Not unconnected with the Cuban matter is the course of events in the Dominican Republic in 1965. Here, for the first time in over three decades, American marines were landed in a Latin American state. At any previous period this action would have aroused virtually unanimous condemnation in the states of Latin America. In this instance, however, several Latin American states cooperated with the United States in restoring public order, and in preparing the way for an election, which was peacefully conducted, and which resulted in June, 1966, in a democratically chosen government.

The story is worth telling in detail. It not only indicates a change of attitude with regard to Latin America revolution in the Caribbean, but it points a moral. For few episodes have aroused more indignation among a certain section of American opinion. Had the critics waited to discover what the result of American action was to be, they might perhaps have made a judgment far less harsh than that which they uttered at the time. But let us examine this matter in its historical setting.

The story is a tangled one, and involves first of all a brief historical review. The Dominican Republic from 1931 to 1963 was governed by one of the most unsavory, if also one of the strongest, of Latin American dictators, Rafael Leonidas Trujillo. Trujillo treated his country as his personal estate; what was more, he incurred the dislike and detestation of other Latin American governments by intriguing against them, especially against Romulo Bétancourt, the very able and democratically-minded President of Venezuela. In 1963 Trujillo was assassinated, and after a period of provisional government Dr. Juan Bosch, a well-known man of letters, was elected to the presidency, in one of the most orderly and one of the fairest elections in the history of the republic. But soon the cycle of disorder that had alternated with dictatorship in the history of this little state reasserted itself. After seven months in office Bosch was overthrown, and a Rightist government under Cabral took office. This regime in its turn was overthrown by a military revolt in which Bosch's supporters played a part. The Dominican state was threatened by civil war. The leaders of the revolt held a part of the city of Santo Domingo; they never controlled the countryside. And they were opposed by a group of Rightists representing the spirit of the old regime. Fighting broke out, the lives of foreigners were thought to be endangered; and requests came from the American embassy for the landing of troops. The first landings, substantial in numbers, took place on the 24th of April, 1965. They were later reinforced until the American government had nearly 20,000 troops on the soil of the republic.

On the 2nd of May President Johnson addressed the nation on the subject. He called attention, very naturally, to the danger to foreign residents implicit in the situation in Santo Domingo City. But, he added, Communist leaders, many of them trained in Cuba, seeing a chance to increase disorder, to gain a foothold, joined the revolt. They took increasing control. And what began as a popular democratic revolution committed to promote social justice was taken over and placed in the hands of a band of Dominican Communists. Many of the original leaders of the revolution, the followers of President Bosch, took refuge in foreign embassies because they had been superseded by other and evil forces. The Secretary-General of the rebels appealed for a cease-fire but he was ignored. The revolution was now in other and dangerous hands.

It is difficult to say whether or not the President's account of events can be accepted. By many of those who witnessed the revolution, particularly by some of the journalists, and especially by the very able reporter, Tad Szulc, of the *New York Times*, the significance of the Communist threat has been depreciated. On the other hand, John Bartlow Martin, the special emissary of the Johnson administration during the crisis, a highly respected figure and a former ambassador to the Republic, believes the danger to have been real. And both Szulc and Martin believe that the President was justified in landing troops, though they differ as to the grounds of such action.

On the other hand it is worth noting that one of the most candid of the critics recognized the necessity of landing the marines, though condemning the operation on broader grounds.

The debate on the propriety of the administration's action that followed the landings assumed in some instances, and especially in the speech which Senator William J. Fulbright delivered in the Senate on September 15, that the administration, in its anti-Communist fervor, had made itself the instrument of reaction. This is certainly not the case. Simultaneously with the landing of the marines, the question was brought before the Organization of American States; the Secretary-General of the Organization, Señor Mora, made a trip to the island, a peace mission followed, and on May 3 a proposal for an inter-American force was put forward. This proposal was endorsed by the Latin American republics on the 6th of May, by a vote of 14 to 5. It is a significant fact that the representatives of every one of the Caribbean republics, with the exception of Mexico, voted in the affirmative. In due course troops from some of the Latin American states took up their station. A Brazilian contingent consisted of 1,500 men; there were also small forces from Honduras and Guatemala, and a token force from Costa Rica.

By this time fighting had largely ceased; after laborious negotiations in which the American representative played a distinguished part, a provisional government was established under a widely respected Dominican, Hector García Godoy. The way was thus prepared for elections, which took place in June of 1966. These elections were remarkable for the respect paid to public order, and they resulted in the peaceable choice of José Balaguer to the office of chief executive. It is, of course, too early to make a truly historical judgment; but in the perspective of 1966 the action taken by the United States and the Organization of American States seems to have promised a more peaceful period in the affairs of this troubled state.

Of course the Russians attempted to make such trouble as they could at the time of the intervention. The action of the American government was made the subject of a debate in the Security Council of the United Nations. The representative of the Soviet Union rang the usual changes on the charge of American imperialism. A resolution was introduced condemning the landing of the marines. Though three states abstained, the only positive votes for this resolution were cast by the Soviet Union and Jordan. The emissaries of the Latin American states would have nothing to do with this maneuver. Moreover, when, some time later, President Johnson visited Mexico he met with an uproariously cordial reception. One wonders if the course of events would have been what it was had not the Russians alienated Latin American opinion by their action in Cuba in 1962.

The fact should be made clear that it is entirely possible, as we have already said, that the Johnson administration exaggerated the Communist danger. But this does not alter the fact that the action taken set a possible new precedent in the event of political disturbance in the Caribbean.

But what of the general question of the danger of Communism in the Latin American area? In the main, the peril has been exaggerated. This is not to say that it is nonexistent. The study of history offers no guide lines for such confident prophecy. The existence of profound social inequalities in most of these states, the depressed conditions of no inconsiderable part of their population, the possibility of a population explosion in some of them (not in all of them), the spirit of nationalism that feeds the spirit of antagonism to capitalism, and especially to American capitalism—all these are factors that cannot be ignored in considering the future. But there are factors on the other side, and they have not, in my opinion, been given the weight they deserve.

In the first place, it is an error to believe that there is only one choice to be made, the choice between Communism and democracy as it is practiced in the United States. The whole history of man refutes this naive view. No society is precisely like any other; each is shaped by a variety of forces, no two instances precisely the same. Communism itself, in the contemporary sense (and to this point I shall return in my last chapter), already shows signs of diversity; to say nothing of the bitter ideological controversy between Russia and China, who believes that the organization of Yugoslavia and the organization of Bulgaria amount to the same thing, or that Castro's Cuba is a little replica of Moscow? Nor does the West exhibit democratic uniformity. Spain and Portugal are still authoritarian states of the Right; there are many authoritarian features in the France of General de Gaulle; there is parliamentary democracy in England, and presidential democracy in the United States. In Latin America, today, there exists an old-fashioned military dictatorship in Paraguay, a Communist régime in Cuba, democratic régimes in Costa Rica and in Uruguay, and a military guardianship of the democratic process in Brazil. We need to understand fully the fact that national temperaments and national pasts are infinitely various, and that these variations will be reflected in governmental forms.

I cannot forbear, in this regard, quoting the profound comment of Winston Churchill on this matter. It will be remembered that when the United States and Great Britain invaded

North Africa in 1942, in the course of the World War, they were faced with the possibility of prolonged French resistance to the landing. To avert this danger, they entered into negotiations with Admiral Darlan, second in command in the regime of Marshal Petain. They did so because they recognized that the French military services were intensely hierarchical in character, and because Darlan was the man whose orders not to resist were most likely to be obeyed. There arose, however, both in Britain and in America, a storm of criticism, and Churchill had to explain his action in the House of Commons. He did so in a pithy sentence. "I entreat the members of the House," he said, "to remember that God in his infinite wisdom did not fashion Frenchmen in the image of Englishmen." Here is an essential truth.

The application of this truth to Latin America does not suggest the future triumph of Communism. It is true that Communist doctrine has been applied with a substantial measure of success (though not with a success comparable to that of the best examples of Western capitalism) in the Soviet Union. But here the circumstances were especially favorable. In terms of natural resources, Russia is one of the most fortunate countries in the world. It possesses ample quantities of the raw materials on which a great industrial society must be based: coal, steel, petroleum and many other products. In such a situation it was possible for Lenin and Stalin to develop their economy on an autarchical basis with relatively little assistance from the outside world. No such situation exists in most of the countries of Latin America. Chile and Venezuela possess important resources from the point of view of industrial growth. So does Brazil. But many of the republics are dependent economies. The phrase should carry no suggestion of denigration. It simply represents a fact. To cut off connections with the West, and to establish close relations with the Soviet Union, would be an act of folly—and is more and more recognized by Latin Americans themselves to be an act of folly. This, of course, is precisely what

Castro has done in Cuba. The results are not such as to encourage imitation. Quite the contrary.

Another advantage that the Soviet Union possessed in its application of Communist doctrine was the character of the Russian people, described by one wise student of Russia as "the most apolitical people in the world." The phrase may be questioned; but no one can deny that the Russians have been habituated to control from the top throughout virtually all of their history. This has not been the case in Latin America. There have been, it is true, many instances of personal rule. But personal rule has practically never been institutionalized. Sooner or later the Latin American authoritarian ruler has been overthrown; sooner or later in most of the states the democratic spirit has contended with the spirit of centralized control. Moreover, it is almost inconceivable that in any Latin American state there should exist the kind of domination of the economy by the government that is the central principle of Communism. Indeed, even the largest and richest republics of the South have had all kinds of difficulties in controlling their economies, have been vexed by the problems of riotous inflation, and by economic disarray, not economic authoritarianism. It is difficult to believe that the Latin American temperament would willingly submit to the kind of dictation from the top that the people of Russia have, in the last century, borne so uncomplainingly.

But there are more powerful reasons than these for believing that Communism will not become the way of life in Latin America. In the most striking cases where a Communist regime has come into power, its advent has been preceded by the collapse of military authority. In 1917 the Bolsheviks entered a vacuum caused by the war-weariness of the Russian people and the disintegration of the Russian armies. In the years following 1945 the forces of Chiang Kai-shek became increasingly demoralized, ill-paid, cooped up in the towns while the Communists roamed the countryside, and fired by no positive social purpose. The result was the triumph of Mao Tse-tung. In Cuba in 1958, as we have already pointed out, the moral rot in the forces of Batista, and the withdrawal of American aid, played an important part in the Cuban revolution.

Is any such pattern likely to be repeated in the countries of Latin America? One would not think so. There are many Latin American countries where the armed forces play an important role in politics. There are some in which this role has been virtually endemic. There are some in which the end result has been a brutal and corrupt dictatorship. But nowhere have these forces been drawn to Communism. Historically, speaking, the military people have usually been the supporters of the local oligarchies. As time has gone on, they have been recruited on a broader class basis. And in recent times they have often played a not unworthy role in promoting that economic stability on which economic progress depends. In Brazil the government of General Branco, established in 1964, has worked valiantly to pull Brazil out of the chaotic situation in which a government which flirted with the extreme Left had left it. In such a state as El Salvador the government of Julio Rivera has been promoting a program of social and economic advance, which is the best antidote to Communism. In the most advanced of the states, in Venezuela and in Mexico, the army has been the sure guarantor of the democratic order. In Guatemala, as we have already seen, the army reacted against the left-wing tendencies of the Arbenz regime.

Another consideration that ought to be taken into account is the increasing social sensitiveness of Latin American regimes. The matter is too large a one to be discussed in detail here. But we shall have more to say of it when we come to discuss the Alliance for Progress.

Finally (and the fact is important), those who live in nervous fear of revolutionary change rarely reflect sufficiently on the toughness of any society, on its strong survival capability. Having lived through two great revolutions, those of us who remember them can understand better than the very young how strong are the forces of resistance to change, how powerful the factors of inertia that militate against drastic alteration of the existing order, particularly in a society in which the economic level is low, education limited, tradition strong, and the dynamic forces limited in scope. A visit to India will make clear to any thoughtful man how massive are the elements that stand in the way of revolutionary change, how divorced from the currents of our own time are enormous numbers of the peasants in the Indian villages. The Guatemalan Indian lives a separate existence of his own, little touched by the conditions of an advanced society. So, too, do many other of the disadvantaged groups in Latin America. They can, on occasion, be roused to violence, but they are not the kind of material out of which a new revolution can be fashioned.

Finally, the Communist doctrine has begun to lose its appeal. The performance of the most powerful of the Communist states, the Soviet Union, falls far behind the performance of the great states of the West. The Communist attitude toward other societies is more and more clearly seen to be a new kind of imperialism, not a gospel of regeneration. The Communist order, in its insistence on the repression of individual liberty, and on the domination of every aspect of life by the state, is increasingly recognized for the evil that it is. We do not need to cower in fear of the future. We do not need to live in constant terror of Communist subversion.

Before turning to our economic relations with Latin America, we should say a word about a question which at all times creates substantial difficulty. This is the question of diplomatic recognition. Should we recognize any government that is in actual possession of the authority of the state? Or should we distinguish between, say, a tyranny like that of Trujillo on the one hand, and a democratic regime on the other? How should we deal with military coups? Wait until the military regime holds a fair election, or deal with it as soon as it has established its position?

The answer to these questions has not been easy, nor has our practice been uniform. Perhaps the best way to deal with the question is to recognize the historical realities. Refusal to recognize a government whose moral origins we dislike has rarely been successful in practice. Sometimes, indeed, it has actually fortified a regime, by making it possible to appeal to the spirit of nationalism against foreign interference. Rarely has it driven a régime from power. On the other hand, we do not need to overdo the principle of recognition of *de facto* governments. We need not express cordiality toward them, or grant them aid as a matter of course, without regard to the policies they pursue. We do not need to embrace them. Probably the best course is to deal with them, but to use our influence to urge a return to legitimacy, that is, to free elections, and to encourage social policies that look in the direction of a better order. Whatever we do, there will be some one to criticize. Democratic theorists will complain whenever we deal with military governments; those of John Birch mentality will think any anti-Communist government is good enough for them. But the middle course is still the safest.

Let us turn from our political relations with the states of Latin America to our economic relations. We have already adverted at the beginning of this chapter to the grievances that the Latin Americans sometimes feel in connection with the United States. This sense of grievance is of long standing, but it was perhaps never stronger than in the late fifties. The United States had been thoroughly preoccupied with the affairs of Europe and of Asia. It had, during the secretaryship of John Foster Dulles, paid relatively little attention to our southern neighbors. The secretary's tone was often patronizing. Occasional sops to Latin American opinion were insufficient. At Caracas, in 1954, the tone of the debates on Guatemala, as we have seen, was hardly flattering to this country. Two events at the end of 1958 pointed up the anti-American feeling. One was Richard Nixon's "good-will" trip to South America. He was the object of violent demonstrations in Peru and in Caracas, in which he bore himself with courage and dignity, but hardly succeeded in allaying hostility. Hard on this visit came the revolution in Cuba. It was beginning to be clear that the times called for a new look at our Latin American policy.

Though the Kennedy administration was to get most of the credit, the "new look" came with the Eisenhower administration. One of the principal complaints of the Latin American states was that the United States took an unsympathetic attitude towards attempts to stabilize the prices of their exports, in particular, coffee. A second complaint lay in the difficulty of securing loans for capital development. There were, it is true, a variety of agencies that dealt with this problem. But the terms of loans were deemed to be unduly difficult, and the number of these loans was scanty as compared with the sums granted to states in other parts of the world.

On both these points the Eisenhower administration made concessions. It took steps to facilitate the working of the International Coffee Stabilization agreement. And it established the Inter-American Development Bank, with a lending capacity of one billion dollars, half of which sum was contributed by the United States. It increased the amount of foreign aid granted to Latin America.

The Kennedy administration went further. At the Inter-American Economic Conference at Punte del Este in the summer of 1961, an ambitious program was drawn up, and approved by the representatives of all the Latin American states except Cuba. Much of this program depended upon the policies of the Latin American states themselves. But in part it was to be financed by the Bank, or other international agencies, and a special fund was created dubbed the Inter-American Fund for Social Progress. A special emergency fund of $150 million was set up for the United States for short-term aid.

Other steps were to follow. By a program initiated in 1961, under certain conditions the American government will guarantee foreign investment against expropriation or deterioration of the currency, by a written contract drawn up, naturally, after careful examination of the project in question. Thus, too, the State Department will pay half the cost of a survey program designed to open the way to specific investment opportunities. Such a survey may include such considerations as the potential market, the location of plants, the availability of raw materials, the profitability of the enterprise, and the potential contribution of the investment to the country's economy. Hopefully one can look forward to increasing use of these forms of encouragement. The popular name for the new policy toward Latin America has been the Alliance for Progress. How has it fared since it was set in motion? The answer is not a simple one.

There have been considerable advances to Latin America, not only from the Inter-American Bank, but from other agencies such as the Export-Import Bank and the International Bank for Reconstruction and Development. The Inter-American Bank alone has approved loans of over a billion and a half dollars since 1961. More than a billion has been allotted in foreign aid. And a substantial part of these loans has gone for the improvement of education, of public health, of housing and other such social purposes. In addition, the cooperation of the United States in stabilizing coffee prices has been very welcome. Moreover, with the encouragement of the United States, the states of Central America have approved a treaty that looks to a common market among these states, and which, in its operation, has been a great success. Still further, eight nations, again with American urging, established in 1961 an American Free Trade area, which looks to the elimination of customs duties over a period of twelve years. These nations are Argentina, Brazil, Chile, Uruguay, Paraguay, Peru, Colombia, and Mexico.

But there have also been grave difficulties, and the results are nowhere near what was achieved by the Marshall plan. It will be remembered that the European nations concerned in the Marshall plan cooperated closely with one another, and carried through important measures looking to fiscal stability and the avoidance of inflation. Moreover, they acted cooperatively in determining what should be the scope of aid from the United States. In the working of the Alliance there have been no such successes. Some of the most important states of Latin America, notably Brazil and Argentina, have been passing through a period of severe inflation. And the agreements made for the implementation of the Alliance have been made with the individual states, with varying success. The scale of the whole operation has been, of course, by comparison much smaller than the tremendous adventure in Europe that was inaugurated in 1948. It is true that our perspective is a short one. It is true that in some of the states, notably Peru under Belaunde, in Venezuela under Bétancourt and his successor, and in El Salvador under Julio Rivera, much progress has been made. It is true that in Brazil, after a period of riotous inflation and irresponsible Leftism, a military government has sought to prepare the way for a more rational economic order. But the difficulties in the way of the development of the Latin American states are many. And, without minimizing the importance of foreign aid, their solution will not come about through the wisdom or the generosity of the United States. It will come about through the efforts of their own statesmen, as it has come about to so large a degree in the Europe of today.

SIX

Today

We must begin this last chapter as we began the first one. The salient fact in the last twenty years, is the development, on the the part of the United States, of a massive military and economic power, of departure from traditional ideas of isolation, of expanding commitments all over the world. The process has transcended the individual human will; no statesman, no group of statesmen, can be said to have planned matters that way. If there is an historical explanation of what has occurred, it lies chiefly in the doctrine of Arnold Toynbee, in "challenge and response." None of the great Western peoples has been less "imperialistic" in its way of thinking; none has been less disposed to dominate others; none has had a more severely civilian tradition. In 1945 the first impulse, as we have seen, was to demobilize our armies, and return to "normalcy," as we did in 1919; without doubt the militancy of the Kremlin did more to bring about American policy in Europe than the purpose of any American statesman. The same irony is present in our policies in Asia; we were, as we have seen, on the verge of withdrawal from the Continent in 1948 and 1949; it was the Korean war that initiated the policy of new commitments in the Orient. Vietnam illustrates the same point. True, our first commitments there were not due to the same kind of direct challenge; but without the North Vietnamese attack on the South, is it likely that we would be building up a powerful base in South Vietnam, and pursuing a policy that binds us more and more closely to the South Vietnamese? Is it not likely that if "Uncle Ho" and his friends had held their hand, they would have been able at some convenient time in the future to bring about union with the South by a process of political penetration?

But whether this thesis of "challenge and response" is true or not the fact of American power is clear. The question we must put to ourselves is the question as to how that power has been used.

Since self-examination and self-flagellation are particularly in the nature of things in a democratic state which still has an uneasy feeling that power is immoral, it is not strange that our current policies have their critics.

In a lecture delivered at Johns Hopkins in the spring of 1966 Senator William J. Fulbright, the distinguished chairman of the Senate Committee on Foreign Relations, expressed grave apprehension as to the trends of American foreign policy, and as to the growth of "arrogance" and the dangers of the abuse of power in the conduct of our affairs. We may well begin by examining the senator's thesis.

A critical attitude with regard to the use of American power must necessarily rest upon one of two assumptions, first, that that power has been used for ends that merit moral condemnation; second, that it has been extended, or rather overextended, so that the burdens assumed had become greater than could be borne. Neither of these statements, at this moment, appears to the writer to be true. In the twenty years since the end of the Second World War, the United States has played a key part in the reconstruction of Europe, to its own advantage and to the advantage of the Western world. As we have already said, we cannot with exactitude declare that it has protected Europe from invasion, but we can say that it has sought to provide a deterrent to invasion, and we can say that there has been no invasion. It has sought to protect the people of free Berlin, and it has protected them. Is there anything in this record for which to blush?

In Asia, the United States has assisted in the recovery of a prosperous Japan. There may be some reservations as to the wisdom of our commitments to the government of Chiang Kai-shek on Formosa, but in economic terms the island is one of the most prosperous parts of the Far East. We should once again stress the fact that an ambitious program of agrarian reform has been carried out there. We cannot foresee the future. The death of Chiang Kai-shek may be followed by unpleasant changes. But in our present perspective we have little to regret, especially if our thoughts turn to the suffering of the Chinese peasant on the mainland in the days of the "great leap forward". In Korea, there exists a government very far from democratic. But there can be no doubt that the South Koreans did not wish to be overrun by the North, and that we assisted in defending them. Are we to expect democratic regimes like our own to flourish in the Orient? Or must we make allowances for differences in background, in national temperament, in economic circumstance? Here again, would it have been better to have stood aside, and permitted South Korea to be overrun? And is the economic situation today worse than it would have been if the invasion from the North had succeeded?

Then there is Vietnam. We are, it is necessary again to insist, involved in an unfinished business. How far we shall succeed in establishing there a viable regime, and in carrying through a program of social renovation, it is, of course, at this moment impossible to say. But we certainly are not in Vietnam to promote our own economic interests, or to exploit the Vietnamese people. On the wisdom of our policy there is room for debate. But is there any "arrogance?"

There is also Latin America. Have we abused our power here? With regard to Cuba, it must be admitted that the Bay of Pigs affair was an error. Since then we have abstained from intervention, in spite of the Communist orientation of the Castro regime, and in spite of vast confiscations of American property. Is there an abuse of power here? In the rest of Latin America, we have, with one exception, used our military power not at all, and in the one case where we have used it, we secured the approval of more than a majority of the members of the Organization of American States. The exception, of course, was the Dominican Republic. Here the facts are confusing, and dogmatism is dangerous. But what was our motive? To secure an honest and free election, to diminish the influence of ambitious generals, and to assist in the encouragement of democratic institutions. As matters stand, peace has been restored; an honest and free election has been held and our forces have withdrawn. The future, of course, is unclear. Whether tranquillity and progress will follow is a matter for the Dominicans. But have we abused our power?

But let us go a bit further. We have been seeking, in our foreign policy, to strengthen a certain form of political and economic organization. We have not sought to prescribe forms of government precisely like our own, or to impose our system on others. We have practiced no narrow economic nationalism. There are few of us today who believe in the laissez-faire of the 1920's. Calvin Coolidge and Herbert Hoover are not the folk heroes of 1966. We do believe, however, that a mixed society, relying on both private initiative and governmental control, is superior to the economy of the Communist states. Are we wrong?

Let us look at the performance of the Soviet Union. In many ways, Russia has made enormous progress. It is undeniable that a strong state has been constructed on the ruins of Tsarism. For fifty years the public order in Russia has not been disturbed. The process of succession to power, always a difficult matter in an authoritarian state, has been carried out without civil disturbance, or a far-reaching domestic convulsion, though not without prescriptions in 1953. The military power has been kept in subordination to the civil power. Soviet legality is more than a name, and is stronger than it was in the days of Stalin. To say this is not to forget the numerous purges or the millions, literally millions, of lives lost in the collectivization of the farms,

or the narrow basis of participation in politics, or the infringe-
ments on the freedom of thought of the citizen, or the restraints
placed on knowledge of what goes on in the outside world. It
is merely to say that in the broad sense the Soviet system has
worked, and that it obviously commands the loyalty of the great
mass of Soviet citizens. To speak of Russia today as a nation of
slaves is to indulge in hyperbole. On the economic side, too, it is
not wise to depreciate the great achievement. In the production of iron ore, Russia stood first in 1963, second in the production of pig iron, third in the production of coal; on the
agricultural side first in the production of wheat, first in the production of sugar, first in the number of milch cows, first in the
number of potatoes. Its national growth rate has been substantial, and until recent years higher than that of the United States.
Nor can we minimize the great achievements on the scientific
side—the development of nuclear power on a grand scale.

But it would be a mistake to imagine that all these successes
flow from the nature of the Soviet system. In some respects,
Russia was favored by fortune. It possessed enormous natural
resources; at the time of the Revolution it had already carried
to a substantial degree of development the technological revolution that is essential to sweeping economic progress; it had a
docile population, one of the most docile among the great peoples, which submitted to drastic measures of control. It is probable that with these advantages, under any system progress
would have been substantial. Against its successes, moreover,
must be set a number of serious deficiencies. The failure of
Russian agriculture to satisfy the needs of the Russian people is
patent, dramatized by the large purchases of wheat which the
Soviet Union has made abroad in recent years. Even more striking is the situation with regard to consumer goods. In this respect the Russians are far behind the West. It is not only that
they have not been able to produce such goods in adequate
quantities, it is not merely that many commodities which the
West considers essential are in short supply; an additional con-

sideration is that the quality of goods is often shoddy. The loud laments of the Russian consumer have penetrated to the outside world, and are compelling a cautious revision of government policy. The contrast between the Soviet performance and the performance of western Europe, making all allowances for the fearful sufferings of the Russians in the war, is still striking. Indeed, the Soviet Union seems today, somewhat timidly and partially, but experimentally, to be trying to re-create a little more of the spirit of private initiative, and of respect for the profit motive, in its bureaucratic economy. The name of Professor Liebermann has become the symbol of this new development.

That Communism is the wave of the future becomes still more doubtful when we examine the performance of the system in other states. Of China it is not easy to make a judgment; accurate analyses are hard to come by; but grave errors have been committed, as even the Communists must admit, and the situation is certainly not rosy. Castro's Cuba does not invite imitation; and here after a period of attempted industrialization, there has been renewed emphasis on sugar culture, the object in earlier days of so much criticism as a dangerously "monocultural" crop. Eastern Europe is moving, but it lags behind the leading nations of the West and here, also, changes in policy are in the making. The position of the Soviet Union as a world leader is not improved by comparison with the free states of the West. That the Communist system, viewed on its merits, can compete effectively against the Western brand of regulated capitalism as it exists today seems extremely doubtful.

The critics of American foreign policy, Senator Fulbright and others, are naturally disturbed by the rigid tone of hostility adopted by some of our citizens toward Communist states. They should be. Emotion and dogma are no substitute for policy. They are often blinding and dangerous. But is this the dominant mood in 1966? Is there not more disposition to find a way to understanding than ever before? Even with regard to Communist China, American public opinion, despite the intransigent manifestoes that come from Peking, seems more disposed than in years to explore the possibility of understanding. As to the Soviet Union, while the ideological quarrel goes on, there are hopeful signs with regard to the future.

Of course the way to understanding is hard. The policy of the Kremlin is plagued by its own dogma. It is still confined within the limits of its own ideology. It is still in some degree insulated from the rest of the world, the product of men who know little at first hand of the peoples of the West. It is still seriously hampered by misjudgments due to its comparative isolation. It still places an exaggerated value on power. And it bears a heavy responsibility for an arms race which could be checked, if not brought to an end, were it not for its obsession with armament.

Yet the picture is not all black. There is some light amid the gloom. Communication between East and West grows. American broadcasts are no longer regularly jammed. Since the Cuban crisis there has been a "hot line" to Moscow, though it has been little used. There has been an agreement with regard to nuclear testing on land, on sea, and in the air. The recent mediation of the Soviet Union between Pakistan and India seems to be the expression of a different spirit from that which Moscow has usually shown. In the past, most of the time Russian foreign policy has incited trouble, has stimulated it, has rejoiced in it. In this case, it seems to have acted in a different context, using its good offices to bring a futile war to an end.

Most striking, too, is the warm welcome accorded to General de Gaulle on his visit to the Russian capital in 1966. It is not that an enormous amount was accomplished in the form of specific agreements that bear on the most thorny questions of international relations. It is rather that there breathes through the Russian communiqué a palpable desire to become a member of the European family, to be accepted in the European community. The talk is of an accord between East and West, of "the creation of conditions necessary for the establishment of an atmosphere of detente," for "normalization."

These lofty professions, of course, are not to be taken as the equivalent of action. When it comes to translating them into meaningful agreements, the way may be hard. The problems, as we shall see, are intractable ones. But the new tone needs to be set beside a fact of massive importance. The Communist doctrine of the not too remote past was that capitalism would destroy itself in war, and that Communism would survive. The Chinese ideologists still talk as if they believed that an international conflagration would be in their interest, and it may be that they do believe it. But not so the Russians. The epoch-making fact of Khrushchev's regime is the revolutionary declaration of the Russian leader that nuclear war would be as dangerous for one side as for the other, and that such a war would be opposed to the interests of both capitalist and Communist states. This declaration might conceivably be received with scepticism as a mere means of lulling the West into a false security, but the caution of Russian policy in practice, the surrender in Cuba, the abandonment of the pressure on Berlin, suggest that when it comes to a matter of vital interest to the West, the Kremlin, if given a fair chance and confronted by resolution, will not press things to an extreme.

Another aspect of foreign policy that may give us hope for the future is the decline in the Kremlin's ability to control those who used to be described as its satellites. Yugoslavia broke away as early as 1948; Khrushchev paid a kind of penitential visit to Belgrade in 1955, and today Tito and his friends act within their own frame of reference, not as the tool of the Kremlin. The disturbances in Poland and Hungary in 1956 did not result in the overthrow of Communism, but the regimes established in both of these countries are certainly not what they were under Stalin. Even more striking is the independence being displayed today by the government of Rumania and its clear desire to control its own economic and military policy.

This tendency may well develop further, and it should be encouraged. It is silly to equate all Communist regimes with the devil. The internal organization of any state is its own business. The question which ought to be asked is how it conducts itself in the international sphere. There is nothing to fear from the former satellites. We ought to develop as good relations with them as we can, to expand trade and cultural intercourse, to encourage them in an independent role. At times Congress has balked at such a policy. But this does not alter the fact that it would be wise.

What of the breach between the Soviet Union and China? Has this been to the Western advantage? Is it likely to widen or to be healed? The present rulers of the Kremlin have somewhat moderated—if not completely abandoned—the bitter polemics with Peking that characterized the later years of Nikita Khrushchev. The rupture of Communist solidarity is clearly painful to them. But long before the quarrel erupted the divergence began to appear. At no time since Stalin has the Soviet Union encouraged—except verbally—Chinese militancy. It actually appears to have discouraged the invasion of India a few years ago. Furthermore, the days of Russian economic assistance to China are behind us. The key fact is the withdrawal of the Russian technicians in China in 1960. There has been no assistance, so far as we know, in the Chinese efforts to develop nuclear weapons. There are border controversies that do something to disturb Russo-Chinese relations. Of course contemporary judgment of the situation does not run all one way. So long as the hope of understanding exists—and it is not yet dead—it operates to stimulate attachment to the Communist ideology, and to give strength to the right wing in the Kremlin. But it seems fair to say that the Russo-Chinese alliance is moribund. The national interests of the two states are not only not identical; they are divergent. While the Kremlin is attempting to adjust itself to the realities, the spirit of fanaticism still reigns in Peking. This does not mean that the differences between Moscow and Peking are entirely to the advantage of the West, or that we should make any effort to exacerbate the conflict. The denunciations that come from the Chinese as to Russian surrender to the West, denunciations that, of course, far exceed the facts, may have the result of stiffening Russian pride as the leading Communist power and may introduce an element of rigidity into Russian relations with the West. But as to genuine cooperation between the two governments, both the opposition of interests and the realities of the military situation must operate to make any genuine alliance a thing of the past.

What of the Russian position in Africa? In Ghana, Nkrumah has been overthrown. In Guinea, the only one of the French African states to sever its connection with France and to declare its complete independence, the regime of Sékou Touré, is moving toward the West. But the picture is a gloomy one for the Kremlin. It is only in certain states of the Middle East, especially Egypt, that the Soviet Union still exerts a very substantial influence.

As to Latin America, we have already discussed the question at some length. We have pointed out the damage to Russian prestige done by the attempt to implant nuclear weapons in Cuba, and the surrender that followed. The situation in Cuba today must make the more reflective minds in the Kremlin wonder about the feasibility—or the desirability—of encouraging revolutions of the Left in this part of the world, of subsidizing them after they occur. It may well be that the long-term effect on Russian policy will be even more important than the failure in this specific case. Financing other states is a dubious enterprise at best; when it comes to attempting to implant a regime inconsistent with the origins and the habits of another people, it can be more than dubious; it can be costly and futile.

In considering the problem of Russo-American relations today one may carry one's optimism a step further. The primary concern of the Kremlin, it would appear, is to satisfy the aspirations of the Russian people for a better economic life. With regard to this problem, as we have already said, Russia is far behind the West. The gulf, no doubt, can be narrowed. But a great war would certainly not be the way to narrow it. A policy of adventure does not at all accord with the true interests of the Soviet Union.

This optimistic view of the Russian posture in international affairs is reinforced by the situation with regard to physical power, that is, by the nuclear stalemate. It is a grim but hopeful fact that the United States and the Soviet Union possess the power to wreak immense damage on one another. We, on our part, have no intention of using our vast—yes, our preponderant —power aggressively. The Kremlin would not dare to do so. Nor, as the Cuban confrontation demonstrates, and still more the retreat on the question of Berlin, is it ready to push things to an extreme. So long as American strength is what it is today, and so long as the dread exists that if the crisis is serious enough, the United States will not flinch, the chances of war are almost nil. The possibilities of a chance encounter have been reduced to almost zero by the advance in technology. The diplomatic procedures of both of the two powers make it hardly likely that a sudden act of passion will bring the world to the brink of massive destruction. The great word of Winston Churchill, that "peace may be the sturdy child of terror" seems true. By the irony of history, man's power of destruction may well point the way to peace.

The matter may be stated another way. Both the United States and the Soviet Union are tending to accept the status quo, or at least not to wish to change it by armed force. Through the erection of the Berlin wall (monstrous as it is), the Russians have put an end to mass emigration to the West, and thus reduced in importance the position of the German capital. On the other hand, the foolish talk here in America about rolling back the iron curtain has been rendered obsolete by the movement in the satellite states toward a somewhat freer economic and political order. Russian and American interests both require peace. There have been many troubles and much violence in the world at large since 1945. But Armageddon has been avoided. The forces that operate to prevent a direct clash are strong.

Such a statement must not be misunderstood. It does not mean that the competition between the United States and the Soviet Union will not continue. It does not mean that the ill will and jealousy that have steadily played a part in the policy of the Kremlin will soon be exorcised. It does not mean that the ideological conflict between the two great superpowers will come to an end. It does not mean that the Kremlin will not take advantage of every opportunity to exploit the troubles of the rest of the world in its own interest. It does not suggest that the United States can relax its efforts to maintain its present ascendancy in the arms race, or play with schemes of compromise which leave the balance more precarious than it is today. It does not mean that we can exclude entirely the possibility of a new challenge such as that which produced the confrontation of 1962. In addition, there are some differences between the United States and the Soviet Union that do not yield to any easy solution. More than twenty years have elapsed since the end of the war. Yet two rival alliances confront each other in the heart of Europe. And the competition in armaments between the United States and the Soviet Union still goes on.

With regard to the alliances, there have been various suggestions. Almost a decade ago, proposals were brought forward for creation of a nuclear-free zone in Europe. The Polish foreign minister, Rapacki, suggested such an arrangement, and the idea was given further currency by the lectures that George Kennan delivered in London in the winter of 1958. But reception of this idea in the West was by no means cordial, and the tone of Russian diplomacy toward the end of the decade did nothing to make acceptance easier. One may well ask whether it is possible (certainly it is very difficult) to arrive at any agreement with regard to armament without first settling the political questions which divide the West and the East in Europe.

The most important of these questions is the question of East Germany. This is a problem that cannot be solved except with the consent of the West German government. No solution can be imposed from the outside. What the Kremlin would like, of course, is recognition of the East German puppet regime by Bonn. But the ideological factor is a powerful obstacle to any such settlement. It is doubtful whether any West German government could accept the idea. A united democratic Germany is and has been ever since the Geneva conversations of 1955 one of the objectives of Western diplomacy. The East German regime was created by force and is maintained by force. To enter into informal relations with it, to trade with it, to develop cultural relations with it, all these things are possible. But to set the seal of positive approval upon it is another matter. In the study of foreign policy, one must admit that the future is always seen dimly, that what is true today may not be true tomorrow. But formal recognition of a government of such dubious moral origins is a difficult matter. As of today, it seems doubtful whether West German opinion, or the public opinion of its allies, would accept any such decision.

To say this is not to give way to complete pessimism. It is possible that in course of time the East German government itself will be modified, both in its economic forms and in its rigid acceptance of one-party rule. In any case, there is no reason why the question should give rise to war. Neither the East nor the West Germans have bellicose intentions; no one is talking of attempting to alter the present situation by violence. There have been many other questions in the field of foreign policy that do not yield to neat solutions; sometimes the provisional and illogical develops remarkable vitality.

The other problem connected with Germany is the problem of NATO. As long as the main body of European opinion desires American forces in Germany it is likely that they will stay there. And, let us repeat it, not even de Gaulle suggests dissolution of the alliance. The question of NATO, of course, is tied up with the question of competitive armaments. That competition has been going on now for almost twenty years. Had the Russians been willing in 1946 to discuss in a constructive spirit the American proposals for the limitation of nuclear power, it is barely possible that something might have been accomplished. Instead, they chose to challenge the United States. In the long period that has elapsed, the momentum of the rivalry has increased. Powerful interests are enlisted behind its continuance. Powerful emotional factors make understanding difficult. And in addition, two other powers have entered the nuclear field, France in the West, and China in the East. There has been no attempt on the part of the United States and the Soviet Union to curb this development. It is true that since 1958 the Russians have offered no encouragement or positive assistance to the Chinese People's Republic in this field, and there is little likelihood that their attitude will change. The danger to the Soviet Union itself from a nuclear-armed China is too great. It is also true that the United States has taken a dim view of France's effort to enter the nuclear club. But the attitude of Washington and of the Kremlin does not suggest a determined effort to stand in the way of the development of nuclear armaments by other powers. The possession of nuclear weapons may become, perhaps it already has become, a symbol of status in the international society.

One need not succumb to unqualified pessimism. The technological and natural resources necessary to the creation of nuclear armaments are very great. It is a long way, for example, from the nuclear explosions in China to the creation of a missile system on a substantial scale. The economic burden involved in any such enterprise is a great one. Even if nuclear armaments become more general, it is still possible to hope that the restraining forces that operate in the case of the United States and the Soviet Union will operate in a wider sphere, and that nuclear weapons will be regarded as insurance rather than as a means of aggression. But at this point we are leaving the field of history for the field of speculation. We are asking—and do not dare answer—whether man is sufficiently reasonable a creature to avoid the perils of passion or a sufficiently prudent creature to avoid the risks of a nuclear confrontation.

With regard to an international limitation of armaments, the situation can hardly be described as cheerful. Discussions on this subject have been going on for nearly two decades. The story is a very tangled one, and cannot be told here in detail. But as matters stand today, many persons would say that the Russians, while using the disarmament question as a propaganda weapon, have never shown any real willingness to face up to the problem. Even if they were more willing to do so, the experience of the past with regard to measures of disarmament does not offer any extravagant reasons for hope.

Let us review the picture in this regard. In the 1920's and at the turn of the next decade, there seemed to be some chance of limiting naval armaments. Indeed, in the treaty of Washington of 1922, the five great naval powers entered into an engagement with regard to limitation of capital ships and aircraft carriers that seemed to bode well for the future. In 1930, by the treaty of London, the three naval powers, the United States, Great Britain, and Japan signed a new treaty extending the principle of limitation to all types of naval vessels.

The limitation of naval armaments was, no doubt, the easiest form of limitation. It is difficult to conceal the instrumentalities of war on the sea. No elaborate system of inspection was required. In addition, the economic climate for arms limitation was favorable. In the days of orthodox finance and balanced budgets, the desirability of curtailing expenditures for armament wore a different aspect from what it does in our own day. In addition to all this, it was possible to construct an arrangement which, by virtually leaving to Japan naval preponderance in the Orient, removed for a brief time the fear in the Japanese mind of an aggressive act on the part of the two great naval powers.

Even so, however, the agreements to which we have alluded did not last long. Japanese militarism could not be satisfied. The treaties were denounced by Japan in 1934, and a hopeful experiment came to an end.

As for land armaments, the question is more difficult and proved insoluble to the statesmen of the period after the First World War. The Preparatory Commission of the League of Nations labored for years on the problem, without arriving at any substantial result. In 1932 a World Disarmament Conference was called at Geneva. All kinds of expedients were discussed. For example, an attempt was made to distinguish between aggressive and defensive armaments. How impossible any such distinction was is best illustrated by the fact that the American delegation, apparently with a straight face and with a total absence of humor, seriously maintained that aircraft carriers were defensive. An attempt to get at the problem by restricting budgets proved to be entirely impractical. The conference failed.

The plain fact of the matter is that no nation is likely to enter into a compact with regard to land armaments that diminishes its relative position or increases the threat to its own security. And when one considers the complexity of the modern weapon system, one can easily see how difficult it would be to come to an agreement that permitted economies but did nothing to disturb or alter the status quo.

Beyond and above this comes the question of inspection. The Russians, despite the vast improvements in espionage and other methods of securing information with regard to the military posture of other states, retain an almost pathological fear of the intrusion of other powers on their own territory. It will not be easy, therefore, to devise any system of inspection that, while satisfying the necessities of securing adequate and accurate information, at the same time takes account of the susceptibilities of the Kremlin. It goes almost without saying, moreover, that China in her present mood, is not likely to enter into an agreement with other states on this matter.

It is, of course, possible that the enormous cost of weaponry will, at some time in the future, impose some restraint on the growth of armaments. But that day is not yet. Though the fact has been little publicized, the American government is at the present time working hard on the problem of the antimissile weapon. Recent press reports indicate that a very large number of subterranean explosions have been carried on since the agreement of 1962 barring other types of tests. It remains to be demonstrated that economic pressures will slow up experimentation in this field. And with regard to the Soviet Union and the Chinese People's Republic, as matters stand it seems possible to extort from the people of these two countries the funds necessary to carry on further development. Here, for the moment, we shall have to let the matter rest.

The question of armaments leads naturally to the question of peace machinery in a nuclear age, and in particular to the place of the United Nations in the world of today. Here a balanced judgment must rest somewhere between those who indulge the warmest hopes for the future, and those who, in disillusionment, wish to depreciate the value of the existing organization.

We have already alluded in a previous chapter to the fact that the collective security arrangements of the Charter have not been successful, and are not likely to be successful. The composition of the Assembly, indeed, makes effective action against an aggressor more improbable than ever. The large number of African nations, comprising more than a third of the total membership, suggests that positive coercive action can hardly be expected. It is the natural and indeed logical objective of these nations to keep out of the competition of the great powers, to benefit when they can by the rivalries of the great states and to confine themselves to statements of high principle, rather than to common measures against an aggressor. This is not to say that the peacemaking machinery of the world institution may not be used at all. The way is open for collaborative action on the part of some of the member states to take steps among themselves where a specific dispute endangers their interest. Under imaginative leadership there always lies open the opportunity to use the Charter in a constructive way, as it was used in the dispute between Egypt and Israel, or in the question of Cyprus, or (despite grounds for criticism) in the Congo. It is merely to say that unanimous action on any question will be difficult to attain.

This is by no means to depreciate the value of the United Nations organization in international affairs. One of its transcendent values lies in the opportunity it provides for quiet consultation on international issues, for continuing contact and for better understanding of the problems of the individual states. Just because this kind of thing is not dramatic is no reason to undervalue it.

Speaking from a more national point of view, the existence of the United Nations in New York offers to the United States a tremendous opportunity to familiarize other nations with the American realities. The image of the United States abroad is often a false one. The immense power that this country wields, the enormous scope of its economic activity, the success—always in comparative terms—of its economic system as compared with the realities of Communism, when witnessed at first hand, have their impact on the representatives of other states. Nor is this all.

The specialized agencies of the United Nations, the World Health Organization, the Food and Agriculture Organization, for example, to mention two of the most conspicuous, provide all kinds of useful materials and suggest all kinds of useful approaches to some of the most difficult and pervasive questions of our time. The statistical data collected in New York open the door to the treatment of all kinds of social and economic problems. We should be much the poorer without them.

Mention of the United Nations leads us to a broad view, not

of the competition of the great powers, but of the many new states that have come into being in the last two decades and that furnish more than a majority of the members of the world society. What are the salient facts that should be borne in mind as we watch the developments of the future?

We may begin by commenting on their political organization. And we shall have to admit in the first place that the chances that they will develop institutions akin to those of the democratic West are not brilliant. Democracy is the most difficult of all forms of political organization. As an abstract proposition it may well be contended that democratic government is that form of government which represents the height of man's political achievement. It makes it possible for every member of society to express and to further his interests within a framework of domestic tranquillity; it settles disputed questions by debate rather than by force, "counting heads instead of breaking them," as the phrase goes; it is based on compromise, and, in an imperfect way, on human rationality, seeking to find a general interest in the welter of conflicting special interests; it is based on faith in the wisdom and the restraint of the average man. But to say these things is not to say that democracy is attainable for all societies; indeed, the study of history suggests that the reverse is true, that in the long history of the race democratic governments have been rare, both in time and in space, and that the actual operation of the democratic system requires unusual qualities of self-restraint, unusual respect for legal forms, and widely diffused intelligence among the members of the political body. Even in the sophisticated Western world, and in the last fifty years, democracy has been set aside, in the Fascism of Mussolini, in the National Socialism of Hitler, in the authoritarianism of Spain and Portugal, and has been put in leading strings in the France of General de Gaulle. It would be too much to expect that the newborn states of Africa or of the Middle East, to mention only the most conspicuous examples, will develop along purely democratic lines.

Indeed, from one angle of view, democracy may be regarded as a consequence of a certain kind of social and economic development. It may be thought of as arising only where property is widely distributed, and where economic independence fosters political self-expression. Many countries most certainly do not fall into this category.

To predict what form of government will arise is another matter. It seems safe to say that military power will play a great role, as it did in Latin America in the nineteenth century, and still does to a substantial extent. But what type of leader will emerge? Who can say? He may be a pure exploiter of the resources of his people. He may be a public -spirited administrator. He may be highly competent in mobilizing what resources are at hand. He may be ignorant and inept. What will there be behind him? Some of the new states have some kind of administrative structure, some form of bureaucracy, on which to build. Some have almost none. In some education is at a minimum. (Tripoli is said to have had three native college graduates in the country when it became independent.) In others some foundation has been laid for an educated class. Will the new states be viable? What of racial strife, a vital factor in one of the most promising, Nigeria? What of competing military groups? What of foreign intrigue?

The bleaker side of the picture can be best understood by taking a look at contemporary Haiti. Haiti declared its independence in 1804. There has been a long time in which to make progress. Yet the government of Haiti today is one of the worst in the world, a tyranny, and an inept tyranny.

We should not, however, allow ourselves to be mastered by pessimism. Once again, to make the Latin American comparison, any observer of the republics which came to birth in the second and third decades of the nineteenth century might well have come to gloomy conclusions. Time has shown that bad regimes may be succeeded by better ones over the long pull.

Nor should we worry about Communism. We have already

stated that Russian stock is very low in the majority of the new states. The example of the leading states of the Western world is far more impressive than that of the Soviet Union. And we may repeat here what has already been said, that such success as the Soviet Union has attained (which must not be depreciated) is due to a combination of circumstances not likely to be paralleled, that is, great natural resources, a considerable technological basis and an effective use of technicians, both Russian and foreign, and an unusually submissive population.

We are led by what has just been said to examine the question of the economic future of the uncommitted states, and to some analysis of Western policy, and particularly of American policy, with regard to them.

We must begin, however, by pointing out that a large number of these states are small, inadequately endowed with natural resources, and in a relatively low stage of educational development. On the roster of the United Nations are a large number of these states, to quote Herbert Feis, "the pinched-in little states of Southeast Asia, the sprawling aggregations of former English, French and Italian colonies in Africa, the smaller Arab components of the former Ottoman Empire, the separated island fragments such as Cyprus, Zanzibar and Malagasy." "A very few of these states can prosper," he adds.

We must also note that over large parts of the world, there broods the specter of Malthusianism, of the increase of population at a rate that exceeds, or nearly equals, the increase in the means of subsistence. I can claim no expert knowledge of the demographic problems of these areas. The easy answer for some persons is birth control. One can agree with the desirability of spreading the knowledge of contraceptive devices, and of simplifying their use, yet be aware of the enormous difficulties that stand in the way of persuading a population of primitive impulses and low cultural attainments to take advantage of such devices. There is, of course, another partial answer to the question of population growth, that is, the improvement of agricultural methods. The United Nations is doing important work in this field through the Food and Agriculture Organization. But here, too, the path is long, and the way is rough.

It is never wise, however, to be drawn into hopeless pessimism by the obstacles in the way of positive policy. The question of assistance by the more prosperous nations to the economically weaker or retarded is one of the great questions of the present day. What can we say about it in this brief chapter?

Before we comment on public aid, we must say a word in support of private aid, that is, the importation of private capital into these states. Marxist dogma describes all such importations as "exploitation" and "economic imperialism." There is no sense to this charge. When a state receives outside capital, it is in a position to tax that capital to its own advantage. If the profits are large, the taxation may be a great source of revenue, and thus of social improvement. In Latin America, today, for example, the most prosperous state is Venezuela. The American interests which have gone there account for no small part of this. The same thing may be said of Mexico. There is another advantage to be drawn from private resources. Private firms bring their technicians with them, and often train the natives to assume a wider control at the same time. This can produce very remarkable results.

But there are difficulties in the way of private investment in the less advanced communities. Capital naturally goes where it can reap the largest rewards and enjoy the greatest security. There are ample opportunities for the venturesome right here at home. American investment in Europe has grown immensely in the last twenty years. Latin America has long attracted American funds. The prospects of reward, therefore, must be very substantial indeed to tempt the American investor to go into the newer countries. The State Department has in some instances been ready to offer special guarantees for investment, as it has done in some parts of Latin America; but this is not an expedient from which a great deal is to be hoped.

There is another reason why private capital cannot be depended upon to do all that needs to be done in connection with the advancement of the underdeveloped nations. A growing economy needs many forms of investment the return from which is indirect. It needs better means of communication; it needs more effective measures against disease; it needs to raise the standard of education; if it cannot provide technicians of its own, as is often the case, it needs to encourage employment of foreign staff. None of these things is private investment in a position to supply, at least directly, and if not connected with its own development program. Of course, a government can, by drastic domestic measures, compel its own citizens to work at low wages; it can operate its own industries, if there is a prospect of development, and use its profits to expand further. This indeed, is the Communist way. But it involves much suffering, and it requires a strong and efficient government. In any case, where natural resources are meager, the level of education low, and competent administrators scarce, development may be very difficult. If funds can be found from public sources, and technical assistance obtained from such sources, the process will at least be easier.

So it is that various international institutions have been growing up since the war to carry a part of the burden of development. So it is that the great nations have found it useful to supply part of the capital needed for growth.

One way of doing this is the grant-in-aid. The brilliant success of the Marshall plan illustrates better than any other case how much can be accomplished by such means. But, as we have already explained, the conditions in this particular instance were especially favorable to success. The countries concerned were mature economies, which needed a push, but which already had many of the elements for reconstruction and growth; they were ready and able to take the necessary steps on their own, to balance their budgets, to reduce tariff burdens, to plan intelligently, and to execute efficiently. That such a success was unusual has been amply attested since that time.

Moreover, when a legislative body is asked to make large appropriations for the benefit of another nation, it is bound to scrutinize with a good deal of care the national gain which is expected to flow from such an enterprise, and although it is dangerous to generalize confidently as to the movement of public opinion, enthusiasm for this kind of assistance seems to be diminishing in the United States. The foreign aid bill enacted in the 86th Congress was not only lower in dollar value than in previous years, but its grants were directed toward a relatively few states.

We come, therefore, to the international institutions for promotion of economic growth in underdeveloped countries. One such institution is the United Nations. But much more important practically are such agencies as the International Bank, the Inter-American Bank, and the International Development Association, to cite the examples in which the United States is especially interested. These institutions are financed by capital grants from the strong nations; control lies in the hands, not of a single power, but of a number of powers; they can be run with genuine expertise, and their decisions carry great weight. When a single nation attempts to give aid, it is bound to append conditions that may prove irksome to the borrower; most of the undeveloped states are sensitive and nationalistic to a degree; they are much less likely to be wounded in their *amour propre* when an international institution makes its judgment on their capacity to use wisely the funds entrusted to them. Of course most of what is given is in the form of loans, but it is possible to vary interest rates greatly, and the International Development Association has been extremely generous in this regard; some credits have been made repayable over a period as long as fifty years, with no repayments at the outset, and with very low rates of interest, or even no interest at all.

It is not the task of the historian to prophesy. We must not imagine that the source of all benevolence with regard to the undeveloped countries is the United States. The French government is today contributing more to various international projects than the American, proportionally to its means. The Colombo plan is an interesting and promising example of international assistance to developing countries. There are reasons for modest optimism. There are pessimists who believe that the richer nations will grow at a rate quite impossible for the newer states, and that they will grow richer as some of the others grow relatively poorer.

We are living, however, in the world of today. Neither extravagant hopes nor exaggerated fears will serve us best in making our own decisions for the future. We shall have to face the grave problems of the international society with enlarged knowledge, with chastened judgment, and with resolution. The dignity of man consists in his effort to improve the milieu in which he lives, and in which his fellows live. As we contemplate the foreign policy of the United States in its broad outlines, there is reason for pride. There is no reason for complacency. The study of foreign policy ought to teach us that we do not control the future of the world. It ought also to teach us to do what we can to see that our own country, in serving its own interest, also serves the interest of mankind.

Bibliographical Note

The literature on American foreign policy since 1945 is massive. What is here intended is merely to point out some of the most essential volumes on the subjects covered by this little book.

GENERAL

Of primary value are the annual volumes published by the Council on Foreign Relations, entitled *The United States in World Affairs*. Of the surveys of American policy on a broad scale the most stimulating, though the briefest, is John Lukacs, *A History of the Cold War* (New York, 1952). Highly useful are William G. Carleton, *The Revolution in American Foreign Policy: Its Global Range* (New York, 1963), and John W. Spanier, *American Foreign Policy since 1945* (New York, 1962).

THE GROWING RIFT

The best account for the whole period 1945-47 is in the relevant volumes of *The United States in World Affairs*. A highly provocative and perceptive discussion of the years 1945-46 is in William H. Mc-Neil, *America, Britain and Russia: Their Cooperation and Conflict* (London, 1953).

Important sources are James F. Byrnes, *Speaking Frankly* (New York, 1947) and Harry S. Truman, *Memoirs* (2 vols., especially vol. 2, *Years of Trial and Hope*, New York, 1955). Of great significance is Joseph M. Jones, *The Fifteen Weeks* (New York, 1955), which deals in detail with the Truman Doctrine.

THE MARSHALL PLAN

For source material see Truman and Jones, and, of substantial importance, *The Private Papers of Senator Vandenberg*, edited by Arthur H. Vandenberg, Jr., and Joe Axel Morris (Boston, 1952). The best secondary account is Harry B. Price, *The Marshall Plan and Its Meaning* (Ithaca, N.Y., 1955), but see also Seymour Harris, *The European Recovery Program* (Cambridge, 1948) and Robert Marjolin, *Europe, the United States and the World Economy* (Durham, N.C., 1953).

For Marshall's secretaryship in general, see the excellent work of Robert H. Ferrell, *George Marshall*, in the series American Secretaries of State and their Diplomacy (New York, 1966).

THE NORTH ATLANTIC PACT

The best work on the Atlantic Pact is by R. E. Osgood, *Nato, The Entangling Alliance* (Chicago, 1962). Another valuable treatment is Alistair Buchan, *Nato in the Sixties: Implications of Interdependence* (New York, 1963). T. W. Stanley, *Nato in Transition* (New York, 1965) and *Facts about Nato*, published by NATO itself (1964) should be consulted. The *Memoirs* of Truman and of Eisenhower are of substantial interest.

THE UNITED STATES AND THE FAR EAST

General works of value are A. D. Barnett, *Communist China and Asia* (New York, 1960) and John K. Fairbank, *The United States and China* (Cambridge, Mass., 1962).

The period of the collapse of the Nationalists is briefly but perceptively treated in Kenneth S. Latourette, *The American Record in the Far East, 1945-51* (New York, 1952). For studies that carry the story down to a later date, see A. D. Barnett, *Communist China: Challenge to American Policy* (New York, 1960) and Harold C. Hinton, *Communist China in World Politics* (Boston, 1966). For the Korean War, see A. M. Schlesinger and Richard Rovere, *The General and the President and the Future of American Foreign Policy* (New

York, 1951) and John W. Spanier, *The Truman-MacArthur Controversy and the Korean War* (Cambridge, Mass., 1959).

On the Vietnam question, the best general guide is by Bernard B. Fall, *The Two Vietnams: A Political and Military Analysis* (New York, 1962).

Outstanding for our postwar relations with Japan is E. O. Reischauer, *The United States and Japan* (Cambridge, Mass., 1965).

THE UNITED STATES AND LATIN AMERICA

The best general work on our relations with Latin America since 1945 is A. A. Berle, *Latin America: Diplomacy and Reality* (New York, 1962). See also Milton Eisenhower, *The Wine is Bitter: The United States and Latin America* (New York, 1966).

On the general problem of American security see J. L. Mecham, *The United States and Inter-American Security* (Austin, Texas, 1960). For the Guatemalan episode, see R. M. Schneider, *Communism in Guatemala* (New York, 1939).

Two accounts of the great confrontation in Cuba of inestimable value are to be found in Arthur M. Schlesinger, Jr. *The Thousand Days* (Boston, 1965) and T. N. Sorenson, *Kennedy* (New York, 1966).

For the Dominican episode, an account for the crucial period of the intervention is Tad Szulc, *Dominican Diary* (New York, 1965).

The best account of the Alliance for Progress is that of J. G. Dreier, *The Alliance for Progress: Problems and Perspective* (Baltimore, 1964).

A general discussion of Communism, not up to date, but useful as giving insight into the problem, is R. J. Alexander, *Communism in Latin America* (New Brunswick, N. J., 1957).

THE CONTEMPORARY VIEW

On Soviet Russia today, a brief but brilliant account is that of Philip A. Mosely, *Russia after Khrushchev* (New York, 1966). The best analysis of the arms problem is J. W. Spanier, *The Politics of Disarmament* (New York, 1964).

On the United Nations, see especially Leland Goodrich, *The United Nations* (New York, 1963) and the pamphlet published by the Foreign Policy Association, *The United Nations Today* (New York, 1965).

On foreign aid, one should read Herbert Feis, *Foreign Aid and Foreign Policy* (New York, 1964) and E. S. Mason, *Foreign Aid and Foreign Policy* (New York, 1964).

For a penetrating discussion of Communism in Africa see I. Brzezynski, *Africa and the Communist World* (New York, 1965).

Index

Acheson, Dean, anecdote on Molotov, 47; and defense of Formosa, 98, 108; and Marshall plan, 43-44; and NATO, 79; quoted on EDC, 83; quoted on Korea, 99; quoted on Russian recovery, 48; relations with Marshall and Truman, 39
Africa, Russia's position in, 161
Alexander of Tunis, Viscount, 17-18
Algeciras, Act of, 69
Alliance for Progress, 49, 150-51
American foreign policy, see U.S. foreign relations
American Free Trade Area, 150
Arbenz, Jacopo, 125, 127-28
Arévalo, President, 125
armaments issue, 165-68
Armas, Castillo, 127, 128
Asia, American policy in, 94-121, 153-54
Atlantic pact, see NATO
atomic energy controls, European Commission for, 65; and nuclear controls, 163, 165-68; U.S. efforts toward international, 30-32
Austrian occupation, 86, 99

Balaguer, José, 142
balance of power theory, and U.S.-Soviet relations, 78-79
Bao Dai, 112, 113
Baruch, Bernard, 30
Batista, Fulgencio, 129-30, 146

Bay of Pigs, 116, 131-32, 154
Belaunde, Victor, 151
Berlin, allied airlift to, 74-77; NATO provisions on, 82; Russia challenges West on, builds wall, 90-92
Bétancourt, Romulo, 140, 151
Bevin, Ernest, 46, 48, 72
Bidault, Georges, 48
Bosch, Juan, 140
Branco, General, 146
Bretton Woods conference, 41-42, 46
Brussels pact, 72-73, 84
Bundy, McGeorge, quoted, 89
Burns, Arthur M., 41
Byrnes, James, diplomacy of, 33; mentioned, 32, 36, 52; negotiations with Russia, 22-25; and postwar Germany, 27-28; quoted on German occupation, 30; and Truman, 39

Cabral (Dominican leader), 140
Cambodian independence, 112
capitalism, aid to new nations by, 173-74; Latin American hostility to, 124
Castro, Fidel, 129-32, 135
Central Intelligence Agency, Bay of Pigs role, 131; Guatemalan action by, 128
"challenge and response" theory of foreign policy, 152-53